LEARN MATH WORKSHEETS

ANSWER KEY

Volume 1

By J.K. Mergens

Learn Math Fast Worksheets Answer Key Volume 1
Copyright © 2021 Registration Number TX 7-316-060
ISBN: 979-8-6983-4141-3
www.LearnMathFastBooks.com

CHAPTER 1

WORKSHEET ANSWERS

LearnMathFastBooks.com

LESSON 1 WORKSHEET

2 + 3 = 5	3 + 2 = 5	3 + 1 = 4	5 + 0 = 5
2 + 2 = 4	3 + 0 = 3	3 + 2 = 5	1 + 2 = 3
5 + 0 = 5	4 + 1 = 5	1 + 4 = 5	3 + 2 = 5

3 + 1 = 4	4 + 0 = 4	2 + 2 = 4	2 + 3 = 5
2 + 2 = 4	2 + 3 = 5	1 + 1 = 2	3 + 2 = 5
1 + 4 = 5	1 + 2 = 3	5 + 0 = 5	1 + 1 = 2

5 - 1 = 4	5 - 4 = 1	5 - 2 = 3	5 - 3 = 2
5 - 5 = 0	5 - 2 = 3	5 - 3 = 2	5 - 1 = 4
5 - 0 = 5	5 - 4 = 1	5 - 5 = 0	5 - 2 = 3
4 - 2 = 2	3 - 1 = 2	5 - 3 = 2	5 - 4 = 1
2 - 1 = 1	1 - 0 = 1	5 - 2 = 3	5 - 3 = 2
4 - 3 = 1	5 - 1 = 4	5 - 3 = 2	4 - 3 = 1
5 - 4 = 1	5 - 2 = 3	4 - 3 = 1	5 - 3 = 2

LESSON 1 WORKSHEET B

1.	1 + 1 = 2	2.	2 + 2 = 4	3.	3 + 3 = 6
4.	1 + 2 = 3	5.	2 + 3 = 5	6.	3 + 1 = 4
7.	2 + 1 = 3	8.	1 + 0 = 1	9.	1 + 3 = 4
10.	5 dogs	11.	3 cats	12.	5 dollars
13.	4 shoes	14.	4 cars	15.	5 toes
16.	5 eggs	17.	5 animals	18.	3 cups
19.	4 cookies	20.	5 minutes	21.	5 books
22.	5 people	23.	4 guitars		

1

LESSON 1 WORKSHEET C

1.	$1 - 1 = 0$	2.	$2 - 1 = 1$	3.	$3 - 2 = 1$
4.	$4 - 2 = 2$	5.	$5 - 3 = 2$	6.	$4 - 1 = 3$
7.	$5 - 1 = 4$	8.	$4 - 0 = 4$	9.	$4 - 3 = 1$
10.	3 dogs	11.	1 cat	12.	3 dollars
13.	2 shoes	14.	1 car	15.	5 toes
16.	1 egg	17.	3 cards	18.	1 cup
19.	0 cookies	20.	1 minute	21.	2 books
22.	1 girl	23.	3 guitars		

LESSON 1 BONUS WORKSHEET

1.	5 Jellybeans	2.	$5 - 3 = 2$
3.	3 Empty stalls	4.	5 cats
5.	1 string	6.	2 puppies
7.	4 years old	8.	$2
9.	5 people	10.	$500
11.	6 miles	12.	5 hours

TEST

ANSWERS 30 SECOND TEST NO. 1

$2 + 3 = 5$	$3 + 1 = 4$	$2 + 2 = 4$	$5 + 0 = 5$
$1 + 1 = 2$	$3 + 2 = 5$	$1 + 2 = 3$	$4 + 1 = 5$
$5 - 3 = 2$	$5 - 2 = 3$	$5 - 4 = 1$	$5 - 5 = 0$
$5 - 1 = 4$	$5 - 4 = 1$	$5 - 2 = 3$	$5 - 3 = 2$
$5 - 0 = 5$	$5 - 3 = 2$	$5 - 4 = 1$	$5 - 2 = 3$

LESSON 2 WORKSHEET

2 + 3 = 5	3 + 2 = 5	3 + 1 = 4	5 + 0 = 5
2 + 4 = 6	3 + 3 = 6	3 + 2 = 5	1 + 5 = 6
6 + 0 = 6	4 + 1 = 5	4 + 2 = 6	3 + 2 = 5
3 + 1 = 4	4 + 0 = 4	1 + 4 = 5	2 + 3 = 5
2 + 2 = 4	3 + 3 = 6	1 + 1 = 2	3 + 2 = 5
1 + 5 = 6	4 + 2 = 6	5 + 0 = 5	3 + 3 = 6
5 - 1 = 4	5 - 4 = 1	5 - 2 = 3	5 - 3 = 2
6 - 4 = 2	6 - 2 = 4	6 - 3 = 3	6 - 5 = 1
5 - 0 = 5	6 - 1 = 5	5 - 5 = 0	6 - 0 = 6
4 - 2 = 2	3 - 1 = 2	5 - 3 = 2	6 - 4 = 2
2 - 1 = 1	1 - 0 = 1	5 - 2 = 3	6 - 2 = 4
4 - 3 = 1	5 - 1 = 4	6 - 3 = 3	5 - 3 = 2
6 - 4 = 2	5 - 4 = 1	3 - 3 = 0	5 - 2 = 3

LESSON 2 WORKSHEET B

3 + 3 = 6	1 + 4 = 5	2 + 4 = 6	5 + 1 = 6	3 + 2 = 5
1 + 3 = 4	4 + 2 = 6	6 + 0 = 6	3 + 3 = 6	2 + 4 = 6
6 - 5 = 1	6 - 3 = 3	6 - 1 = 5	6 - 2 = 4	5 - 4 = 1
5 - 2 = 3	5 - 1 = 4	6 - 4 = 2	5 - 2 = 3	5 - 3 = 2

3 eggs

Even number

$6

6 points

$2

3 petals

5 people on the bus

3 cookies

$4

2

$2 + 4 = 6$	$2 + 3 = 5$	$5 + 1 = 6$	$2 + 4 = 6$
$1 + 4 = 5$	$5 + 1 = 6$	$3 + 2 = 5$	$0 + 5 = 5$
$3 + 3 = 6$	$2 + 2 = 4$	$2 + 1 = 3$	$4 + 2 = 6$
$3 + 2 = 5$	$6 + 0 = 6$	$4 + 1 = 5$	$1 + 3 = 4$
$1 + 5 = 6$	$2 + 3 = 5$	$3 + 3 = 6$	$2 + 2 = 4$
$4 + 2 = 6$	$3 + 1 = 4$	$4 + 2 = 6$	$6 + 0 = 6$
$6 - 1 = 5$	$5 - 3 = 2$	$4 - 2 = 2$	$6 - 3 = 3$
$6 - 5 = 1$	$6 - 2 = 4$	$4 - 3 = 1$	$6 - 4 = 2$
$4 - 1 = 3$	$5 - 4 = 1$	$3 - 2 = 1$	$5 - 2 = 3$
$2 - 2 = 0$	$6 - 6 = 0$	$6 - 3 = 3$	$5 - 3 = 2$
$6 - 2 = 4$	$4 - 0 = 4$	$4 - 2 = 2$	$5 - 2 = 3$
$6 - 3 = 3$	$2 - 1 = 1$	$6 - 4 = 2$	$6 - 2 = 4$
$5 - 4 = 1$	$5 - 3 = 2$	$3 - 3 = 0$	$6 - 5 = 1$

TEST

$3 + 3 = 6$	$2 + 3 = 5$	$4 + 2 = 6$	$5 + 1 = 6$
$3 + 2 = 5$	$2 + 4 = 6$	$4 + 1 = 5$	$3 + 3 = 6$
$6 - 5 = 1$	$5 - 3 = 2$	$6 - 4 = 2$	$6 - 3 = 3$
$5 - 2 = 3$	$6 - 2 = 4$	$6 - 1 = 5$	$5 - 4 = 1$
$2 + 2 = 4$	$3 + 3 = 6$	$2 + 3 = 5$	$3 + 2 = 5$

LESSON 3 WORKSHEET

4 + 3 = 7	3 + 2 = 5	4 + 2 = 6	5 + 2 = 7
2 + 4 = 6	3 + 4 = 7	6 + 1 = 7	1 + 4 = 5
5 + 2 = 7	7 + 0 = 7	4 + 3 = 7	3 + 2 = 5
5 + 1 = 6	4 + 2 = 6	6 + 1 = 7	3 + 3 = 6
2 + 5 = 7	4 + 3 = 7	2 + 3 = 5	1 + 6 = 7
4 + 2 = 6	2 + 2 = 4	3 + 3 = 6	4 + 3 = 7
6 + 1 = 7	5 + 2 = 7	7 + 0 = 7	4 + 1 = 5

7 - 1 = 6	7 - 4 = 3	7 - 2 = 5	7 - 3 = 4
6 - 4 = 2	6 - 2 = 4	6 - 3 = 3	6 - 5 = 1
5 - 0 = 5	5 - 2 = 3	5 - 3 = 2	5 - 1 = 4
4 - 2 = 2	6 - 2 = 4	7 - 3 = 4	5 - 2 = 3
3 - 3 = 0	4 - 1 = 5	6 - 5 = 1	7 - 2 = 5
7 - 5 = 2	6 - 3 = 3	5 - 4 = 1	7 - 6 = 1
4 - 3 = 1	5 - 3 = 2	6 - 4 = 2	7 - 2 = 5

Circle the odd numbers in this row: 6   2

LESSON 3 WORKSHEET B

3 + 3 = 6	2 + 2 = 4	3 + 2 = 5	4 + 2 = 6
3 + 4 = 7	2 + 4 = 6	3 + 1 = 4	5 + 2 = 7
3 + 2 = 5	5 + 0 = 5	6 + 1 = 7	3 + 3 = 6
2 + 5 = 7	4 + 2 = 6	5 + 1 = 6	1 + 4 = 5
2 + 3 = 5	4 + 3 = 7	2 + 2 = 4	1 + 2 = 3

6 cats	7 hamburgers	7 dollars	5 pillows
6 people	7 Plates	6 presents	

3

LESSON 3 WORKSHEET C

5 − 1 = 4	6 − 4 = 2	5 − 2 = 3	7 − 4 = 3
5 − 4 = 1	7 − 2 = 5	5 − 3 = 2	7 − 5 = 2
6 − 0 = 6	6 − 2 = 4	7 − 3 = 4	4 − 1 = 3
6 − 2 = 4	6 − 4 = 2	7 − 1 = 6	5 − 3 = 2
4 − 4 = 0	4 − 2 = 2	6 − 3 = 3	7 − 6 = 1
6 − 5 = 1	6 − 1 = 5	5 − 2 = 3	7 − 5 = 2
2 cans	5 pizzas	2 snowballs	1 foot
5 times	3 video games	4 plates	

LESSON 3 BONUS WORKSHEET

4 + 4 = 8	6 + 2 = 8	4 + 2 = 6	5 + 2 = 7
2 + 6 = 8	3 + 5 = 8	7 + 1 = 8	1 + 5 = 6
5 + 2 = 7	7 + 0 = 7	4 + 3 = 7	3 + 2 = 5
3 + 3 = 6	3 + 4 = 7	5 + 3 = 8	2 + 5 = 7
+ 2 = 4	4 + 4 = 8	3 + 3 = 6	2 + 3 = 5
4 + 3 = 7	4 + 1 = 5	6 + 2 = 8	7 + 1 = 8
2 + 5 = 7	4 + 2 = 6	5 + 3 = 8	7 + 0 = 7
6 + 1 = 7	3 + 2 = 5	1 + 5 = 6	0 + 8 = 8
8 − 1 = 7	8 − 4 = 4	8 − 2 = 6	8 − 3 = 5
7 − 4 = 3	7 − 2 = 5	7 − 3 = 4	7 − 5 = 2
6 − 4 = 2	6 − 3 = 3	6 − 5 = 1	6 − 2 = 4
5 − 0 = 5	5 − 2 = 3	5 − 3 = 2	5 − 1 = 4
4 − 3 = 1	8 − 5 = 3	3 − 2 = 1	6 − 2 = 4
7 − 3 = 4	8 − 4 = 4	6 − 3 = 3	8 − 3 = 5

30 SECOND TEST NO. 3

3 + 2 = 5	3 + 4 = 7	2 + 4 = 6	5 + 2 = 7
6 + 1 = 7	2 + 3 = 5	3 + 3 = 6	4 + 3 = 7
5 + 2 = 7	2 + 4 = 6	2 + 5 = 7	4 + 1 = 5
7 - 2 = 5	7 - 3 = 4	6 - 4 = 2	5 - 3 = 2
6 - 3 = 3	7 - 5 = 2	5 - 2 = 3	6 - 4 = 2

LESSON 4 WORKSHEET

4 + 4 = **8**	6 + 2 = **8**	4 + 2 = **6**	5 + 2 = **7**
2 + 6 = **8**	3 + 5 = **8**	7 + 1 = **8**	1 + 5 = **6**
5 + 2 = **7**	7 + 0 = **7**	4 + 3 = **7**	3 + 2 = **5**
3 + 3 = **6**	3 + 4 = **7**	5 + 3 = **8**	2 + 5 = **7**
2 + 2 = **4**	4 + 4 = **8**	3 + 3 = **6**	2 + 3 = **5**
4 + 3 = **7**	4 + 1 = **5**	6 + 2 = **8**	7 + 1 = **8**
2 + 5 = **7**	4 + 2 = **6**	5 + 3 = **8**	7 + 0 = **7**
6 + 1 = **7**	3 + 2 = **5**	1 + 5 = **6**	0 + 8 = **8**
8 - 1 = **7**	8 - 4 = **4**	8 - 2 = **6**	8 - 3 = **5**
7 - 4 = **3**	7 - 2 = **5**	7 - 3 = **4**	7 - 5 = **2**
6 - 4 = **2**	6 - 3 = **3**	6 - 5 = **1**	6 - 2 = **4**
5 - 0 = **5**	5 - 2 = **3**	5 - 3 = **2**	5 - 1 = **4**
4 - 3 = **1**	8 - 5 = **3**	3 - 2 = **1**	6 - 2 = **4**
7 - 3 = **4**	8 - 4 = **4**	6 - 3 = **3**	8 - 3 = **5**

4

2 + 5 = 7	5 + 3 = 8	5 + 2 = 7	2 + 6 = 8
2 + 3 = 5	4 + 4 = 8	1 + 7 = 8	4 + 2 = 6
3 + 3 = 6	5 + 2 = 7	3 + 5 = 8	4 + 3 = 7
6 + 1 = 7	7 + 1 = 8	6 + 2 = 8	1 + 4 = 5
5 + 3 = 8	8 + 0 = 8	3 + 1 = 4	1 + 2 = 3
4 + 4 = 8	2 + 6 = 8	3 + 4 = 7	2 + 5 = 7
8 - 1 = 7	8 - 3 = 5	8 - 2 = 6	8 - 4 = 4
8 - 6 = 2	8 - 5 = 3	7 - 3 = 4	7 - 5 = 2
7 - 1 = 6	5 - 3 = 2	5 - 4 = 1	6 - 2 = 4
8 - 2 = 6	6 - 4 = 2	8 - 3 = 5	6 - 3 = 3
7 - 2 = 5	8 - 0 = 8	5 - 2 = 3	8 - 2 = 6
6 - 5 = 1	7 - 1 = 6	8 - 4 = 4	8 - 3 = 5
6 - 4 = 2	7 - 3 = 4	6 - 3 = 3	8 - 5 = 3

LESSON 4 WORKSHEET C

4 + 3 = 7	5 + 2 = 7	6 + 2 = 8	4 + 2 = 6
2 + 3 = 5	3 + 4 = 7	7 + 1 = 8	4 + 4 = 8
5 + 3 = 8	6 + 0 = 6	4 + 1 = 5	3 + 2 = 5
3 + 4 = 7	3 + 5 = 8	4 + 3 = 7	2 + 6 = 8
2 + 5 = 7	3 + 4 = 7	5 + 3 = 8	3 + 3 = 6
4 + 4 = 8	7 + 1 = 8	4 + 2 = 6	6 + 1 = 7
2 + 6 = 8	4 + 3 = 7	1 + 3 = 4	7 + 1 = 8
6 + 2 = 8	3 + 5 = 8	2 + 5 = 7	0 + 8 = 8
7 rocks	8	6 points	8 years old
3 pieces of pizza		8 feet	

LESSON 4 BONUS WORKSHEET

4 + 4 = 8	**2** + 6 = 8	5 + **3** = 8	2 + **6** = 8
4 + 3 = 7	4 + 4 = 8	3 + 3 = 6	2 + 3 = 5
3 + 5 = 8	2 + 2 = 4	2 + 6 = 8	3 + 4 = 7
5 + 2 = 7	2 + 4 = 6	8 - 2 = 6	8 - 4 = 4
8 - 3 = 5	8 - 5 = 3	8 - 1 = 7	7 - 4 = 3
6 - 2 = 4	8 - 6 = 2	7 - 3 = 4	5 - 3 = 2

8 is an even number

LOCK COMBINATIONS:

4, 2, **2**	3, 2, **3**	1, 6, **1**	5, **2**, 1
3, 4, **1**	7, 0, **1**	2, 4, **2**	5, **1**, 2
4, 0, **4**	3, 1, **4**	3, 5, **0**	6 , 0, **2**
4, 4, **0**	2, 1, **5**	5, 1, **2**	1, 4, **3**
0, **0**, 8	2, 5, 1	6, 1, **1**	2, 3, **3**

TEST

30 SECOND TEST NO. 4

5 + 3 = 8	4 + 2 = 6	2 + 3 = 5	4 + 4 = 8
2 + 5 = 7	6 + 2 = 8	3 + 3 = 6	4 + 3 = 7
4 + 2 = 6	4 + 1 = 5	3 + 5 = 8	3 + 2 = 5
6 - 4 = 2	7 - 3 = 4	8 - 5 = 3	5 - 3 = 2
8 - 2 = 6	6 - 3 = 3	7 - 2 = 5	8 - 6 = 2

5

LESSON 5 WORKSHEET

5 + 4 = 9	6 + 3 = 9	7 + 2 = 9	5 + 2 = 7
3 + 6 = 9	3 + 5 = 8	7 + 1 = 8	4 + 5 = 9
7 + 2 = 9	9 + 0 = 9	8 + 1 = 9	6 + 2 = 8
6 + 3 = 9	5 + 4 = 9	3 + 3 = 6	2 + 4 = 6
2 + 6 = 8	3 + 4 = 7	6 + 3 = 9	5 + 3 = 8
4 + 2 = 6	7 + 2 = 9	3 + 6 = 9	5 + 4 = 9
1 + 8 = 9	0 + 9 = 9	2 + 2 = 4	4 + 4 = 8
3 + 3 = 6	4 + 2 = 6	7 + 1 = 8	2 + 6 = 8
9 - 1 = 8	9 - 4 = 5	9 - 2 = 7	9 - 3 = 6
9 - 5 = 4	9 - 6 = 3	9 - 7 = 2	9 - 1 = 8
9 - 4 = 5	9 - 3 = 6	7 - 5 = 2	9 - 2 = 7
8 - 4 = 4	8 - 5 = 3	7 - 3 = 4	6 - 2 = 4
5 - 3 = 2	7 - 4 = 3	6 - 3 = 3	9 - 7 = 2
8 - 3 = 5	7 - 5 = 2	8 - 2 = 6	9 - 6 = 3

LESSON 5 WORKSHEET B

4 + 4 = 8	7 + 2 = 9	5 + 4 = 9	3 + 2 = 5
3 + 6 = 9	3 + 3 = 6	5 + 2 = 7	3 + 5 = 8
8 + 1 = 9	6 + 0 = 6	7 + 2 = 9	3 + 4 = 7
4 + 2 = 6	5 + 4 = 9	2 + 2 = 4	6 + 1 = 7
3 + 6 = 9	1 + 4 = 5	3 + 5 = 8	2 + 3 = 5
5 + 2 = 7	2 + 7 = 9	3 + 5 = 8	4 + 4 = 8
0 + 9 = 9	3 + 4 = 7	3 + 5 = 8	5 + 4 = 9
2 + 3 = 5	4 + 3 = 7	6 + 3 = 9	7 + 2 = 9
9 - 2 = 7	9 - 3 = 6	7 + 1 = 8	9 - 6 = 3
9 - 4 = 5	9 - 1 = 8	9 - 7 = 2	9 - 5 = 4
9 - 8 = 1	9 - 2 = 7	9 - 0 = 9	8 - 2 = 6
8 - 5 = 3	8 - 4 = 4	7 - 3 = 4	6 - 4 = 2
5 - 2 = 3	5 - 3 = 2	7 - 5 = 2	9 - 6 = 3
8 - 6 = 2	7 - 5 = 2	7 - 2 = 5	9 - 4 = 5

LESSON 5 WORKSHEET C

1.	9 numbers	2.	5 lives	3.	6 dolls
4.	2 pages	5.	8 toys	6.	9 is odd

MATHWORDS PUZZLE

ANSWERS:

Across:	DOWN:
1. EIGHT	1. EVEN
5. TWO	2. TWO
8. ODD	3. ADDITION
9. NINE	4. EQUAL
10. FIVE	5. THREE
12. XYZ	6. ONE
14. FIVE	7. ONE
16. SEVEN	11. SIX
17. OX	12. PLUS
18. SIX	13. EVEN
19. NUMBERS	14. FOUR
22. ONE	15. EIGHT
23. THREE	16. SIXCARS
24. TEN	29. MINUS
25. SEVEN	21. SEVEN
	23. TWO
	24. TEN

TEST

30 SECOND TEST NO. 5

5 + 3 = 8	6 + 3 = 9	3 + 4 = 7	5 + 4 = 9
3 + 2 = 5	4 + 2 = 6	7 + 2 = 9	3 + 6 = 9
8 + 1 = 9	4 + 4 = 8	2 + 3 = 5	3 + 3 = 6
2 + 5 = 7	6 + 2 = 8	3 + 6 = 9	4 + 5 = 9
9 − 5 = 4	9 − 3 = 6	9 − 6 = 3	9 − 2 = 7

6

6 + 4 = 10	5 + 5 = 10	4 + 4 =8	3 + 3 = 6
7 + 3 = 10	8 + 2 = 10	2 + 7 = 9	9 + 1 = 10
5 + 3 = 8	3 + 4 = 7	6 + 2 = 8	5 + 4 = 9
4 + 2 = 6	6 + 3 = 9	6 + 4 = 10	8 + 2 = 10
3 + 6 = 9	8 + 2 = 10	6 + 1 = 7	3 + 5 = 8
7 + 3 = 10	9 + 1 = 10	8 + 2 = 10	5 + 2 = 7
4 + 3 = 7	5 + 5 = 10	3 + 3 = 6	4 + 4 = 8
2 + 3 = 5	4 + 6 = 10	4 + 3 = 7	3 + 7 = 10
5 + 4 = 9	8 + 2 = 10	5 + 5 = 10	3 + 6 = 9
10 - 5 = 5	10 - 6 = 4	10 - 7 = 3	10 - 2 = 8
10 - 1 = 9	10 - 4 = 6	10 - 8 = 2	10 - 3 = 7
9 - 4 = 5	10 - 2 = 8	7 - 3 = 4	6 - 5 = 1
6 - 4 = 2	8 - 3 = 5	6 - 3 = 3	6 - 1 = 5
9 - 0 = 9	9 - 2 = 7	10 - 3 = 7	5 - 3 = 2
8 - 5 = 3	8 - 7 = 1	8 - 6 = 2	8 - 3 = 5

LESSON 6 WORKSHEET B

1.	8 wheels	2.	5 dolphins	3.	4 more times
4.	7 hours	5.	5 times	6.	10 people

LESSON 6 WORKSHEET C

6 + **4** = 10	7 + **3** = 10	2 + **8** = 10	**5** + 5 = 10
8 + **2** = 10	9 + **1** = 10	3 + **7** = 10	4 + **6** = 10
10 - **9** = 1	10 - **6** = 4	10 - **7** = 3	10 - **8** = 2
10 - **4** = 6	10 - **2** = 8	10 - **5** = 5	10 - **3** = 7
7 + 3 = **10**	**2** + 8 = 10	0 + **10** = 10	**5** + 5 = 10

Your Score	Their Score
6	**4**

Your Score	Their Score
7	**3**

Your Score	Their Score
8	**2**

Your Score	Their Score
4	**6**

TEST

30 SECOND TEST NO. 6

$5 + 5 = 10$ $6 + 2 = 8$ $4 + 6 = 10$ $5 + 3 = 8$

$2 + 8 = 10$ $3 + 7 = 10$ $4 + 3 = 7$ $5 + 2 = 7$

$4 + 2 = 6$ $5 + 4 = 9$ $9 + 1 = 10$ $6 + 4 = 10$

$3 + 6 = 9$ $7 + 2 = 9$ $3 + 3 = 6$ $3 + 2 = 5$

$10 - 6 = 4$ $10 - 7 = 3$ $10 - 2 = 8$ $10 - 3 = 7$

7

5 + 5 = 10	6 + 6 = 12	7 + 7 = 14	2 + 2 = 4
3 + 3 = 6	8 + 8 = 16	1 + 1 = 2	4 + 4 = 8
2 + 2 = 4	0 + 0 = 0	6 + 6 = 12	5 + 5 = 10
3 + 3 = 6	4 + 4 = 8	7 + 7 = 14	2 + 2 = 4

16 - 8 = 8	14 - 7 = 7	12 - 6 = 6	10 - 5 = 5
8 - 4 = 4	6 - 3 = 3	4 - 2 = 2	2 - 1 = 1

7 + 7 = 14	**4 + 4** = 8	**5 + 5** = 10	**6+ 6** = 12
2 + 2 = 4	**8 + 8** = 16	**1 + 1** = 2	**3 + 3** = 6

5 + 5 = 10	2 + 2 = 4	8 + 8 = 16	7 + 7 = 14
6 + 6 = 12	4 + 4 = 8	1 + 1 = 2	3 + 3 = 6

LESSON 7 WORKSHEET B

1. 14 badges	2. 8 dollars	3. 8 Action figures
4. 10 dollars	5. 4 pets	6. 6 miles
7. 12 minutes	8. 2 cartwheels	

LESSON 7 WORKSHEET C

8 - 4 = 4	6 - 5 = 1	8 - 3 = 5	7 - 5 = 2
16 - 8 = 8	14 - 7 = 7	8 - 6 = 2	6 - 4 = 2
12 - 6 = 6	5 - 3 = 2	10 - 5 = 5	7 - 3 = 4
8 - 4 = 4	5 - 2 = 3	6 - 3 = 3	4 - 2 = 2
5 - 1 = 4	7 - 2 = 5	4 - 1 = 3	12 - 6 = 6
8 - 5 = 3	6 - 2 = 4	7 - 4 = 3	14 - 7 = 7
5 - 3 = 2	4 - 2 = 2	6 - 3 = 3	12 - 6 = 6

Continue...

3 + 5 = 8	5 + 5 = 10	7 + 1 = 8	2 + 2 = 4
8 + 8 = 16	4 + 2 = 6	7 + 7 = 14	3 + 4 = 7
6 + 2 = 8	1 + 4 = 5	6 + 6 = 12	3 + 2 = 5
4 + 4 = 8	2 + 5 = 7	6 + 1 = 7	3 + 1 = 4
5 + 5 = 10	1 + 7 = 8	8 + 0 = 8	4 + 2 = 6
3 + 2 = 5	3 + 5 = 8	2 + 6 = 8	3 + 3 = 6
4 + 3 = 7	1 + 7 = 8	8 + 8 = 16	2 + 2 = 4
6 + 1 = 7	6 + 2 = 8	2 + 3 = 5	5 + 2 = 7

TEST

ONE MINUTE TEST NO. 7

2 + 3 = 5	4 + 5 = 9	3 + 3 = 6	5 + 2 = 3	3 + 6 = 9	4 + 2 = 6
5 + 3 = 8	6 + 2 = 8	7 + 3 = 10	5 + 5 = 10	6 + 4 = 10	4 + 3 = 7
3 + 6 = 9	5 + 2 = 7	4 + 2 = 6	4 + 4 = 8	2 + 7 = 9	8 + 2 = 10
2 + 3 = 5	3 + 3 = 6	9 + 1 = 10	5 + 4 = 9	8 + 1 = 9	6 + 3 = 9
10 - 6 = 4	9 - 5 = 4	8 - 3 = 5	10 - 3 = 7	7 - 5 = 2	6 - 4 = 2
8 - 2 = 6	7 - 3 = 4	9 - 6 = 3	10 - 5 = 5	6 - 2 = 4	10 - 4 = 6
9 - 3 = 6	8 - 4 = 4	7 - 2 = 5	8 - 5 = 3	10 - 7 = 3	9 - 2 = 7

Review

1	$5 + 5 = 10$	2.	$2 + 3 = 5$	3.	$1 + 6 = 7$
4.	$3 + 1 = 4$	5.	$5 + 3 = 8$	6.	$2 + 2 = 4$
7.	$8 + 1 = 9$	8.	$4 + 2 = 6$	9.	$7 + 3 = 10$
10.	$4 + 6 = 10$	11.	$2 + 5 = 7$	12.	$3 + 4 = 7$
13.	$3 + 3 = 6$	14.	$3 + 6 = 9$	15.	$4 + 5 = 9$
16.	$1 + 9 = 10$	17.	$2 + 7 = 9$	18.	$8 + 2 = 10$

8 slices of pizza

19.	$3 - 2 = 1$	20.	$10 - 5 = 5$	21.	$5 - 2 = 3$
22.	$10 - 3 = 7$	23.	$8 - 5 = 3$	24.	$10 - 9 = 1$
25.	$6 - 4 = 2$	26.	$9 - 6 = 3$	27.	$7 - 3 = 4$
28.	$10 - 7 = 3$	29.	$4 - 1 = 3$	30.	$5 - 0 = 5$
31.	$8 - 4 = 4$	32.	$7 - 2 = 5$	33.	$8 - 6 = 2$
34.	$10 - 2 = 8$	35.	$10 - 8 = 2$	36.	$7 - 5 = 2$

4 flowers

CHAPTER 1 TEST

1.	6 + 3 = 9	2.	4 + 5 = 9	3.	3 + 4 = 7
4.	5 + 2 = 7	5.	3 + 2 = 5	6.	4 + 6 = 10
7.	7 + 2 = 9	8.	3 + 5 = 8	9.	4 + 4 = 8
10.	5 + 1 = 6	11.	5 + 5 = 10	12.	6 + 2 = 8
13.	3 + 3 = 6	14.	7 + 3 = 10	15.	1 + 6 = 7
16.	2 + 2 = 4	17.	4 + 0 = 4	18.	5 + 4 = 9
19.	8 + 2 = 10	20.	2 + 4 = 6	21.	3 + 6 = 9

22.	10 - 4 = 6	23.	10 - 7 = 3	24.	10 - 8 = 2
25.	8 - 4 = 4	26.	7 - 2 = 5	27.	6 - 3 = 3
28.	10 - 3 =7	29.	8 - 5 = 3	30.	9 - 4 = 5
31.	7 - 4 = 3	32.	6 - 2 = 4	33.	5 - 3 = 2
34.	10 - 2 = 8	35.	9 - 6 = 3	36.	7 - 5 = 2
37.	8 - 3 = 5	38.	6 - 4 = 2	39.	5 - 2 = 3
40.	10 - 5 = 5	41.	9 - 5 = 4	42.	8 - 6 = 2
43.	7 - 3 = 4	44.	5 - 4 = 1	45.	10 - 6 = 4

CHAPTER 2
WORKSHEET
ANSWERS

LearnMathFastBooks.com

LESSON 8 WORKSHEET

7 + 4 = 11	8 + 3 = 11	7 + 5 = 12	8 + 5 = 13
6 + 7 = 13	7 + 7 = 14	8 + 6 = 14	8 + 4 = 12
9 + 3 = 12	9 + 2 = 11	6 + 5 = 11	6 + 6 = 12
8 + 7 = 15	9 + 5 = 14	6 + 8 = 14	7 + 7 = 14
9 + 6 = 15	4 + 8 = 12	7 + 3 = 10	8 + 8 = 16
9 + 9 = 18	8 + 2 = 10	8 + 9 = 17	7 + 9 = 16
5 + 7 = 12	9 + 5 = 14	8 + 6 = 14	5 + 8 = 13
7 + 6 = 13	8 + 4 = 12	6 + 6 = 12	5 + 9 = 14
8 + 5 = 13	7 + 5 = 12	8 + 6 = 14	9 + 7 = 16
8 + 7 = 15	6 + 8 = 14	5 + 9 = 14	3 + 8 = 11
6 + 5 = 11	7 + 6 = 13	4 + 7 = 11	8 + 4 = 12
9 + 3 = 12	5 + 8 = 13	7 + 5 = 12	2 + 9 = 11
7 + 8 = 15	6 + 8 = 14	8 + 9 = 17	5 + 9 = 14
8 + 5 = 13	3 + 6 = 9	4 + 7 = 11	3 + 5 = 8

LESSON 8 WORKSHEET B

1.	16 dolls	2.	16 toy cars	3.	8 whole seashells
4.	13 baked goods	5.	9 snaps	6.	20 whiskers
7.	7 dollars				

LESSON 8 WORKSHEET C

1.   10 points
2.   Seattle won the ball game.
3.   The phone rang 15 times.
4.   14 more wheels
5.   7 gold charms
6.   20 stars
7.   Rocky missed the ball 8 times

TEST

40 SECOND TEST NO. 8

$7 + 8 = 15$	$6 + 7 = 13$	$8 + 5 = 13$	$9 + 7 = 16$
$8 + 6 = 14$	$4 + 7 = 11$	$9 + 6 = 15$	$7 + 5 = 12$
$6 + 5 = 11$	$9 + 8 = 17$	$8 + 4 = 12$	$8 + 8 = 16$
$6 + 6 = 12$	$8 + 7 = 15$	$5 + 8 = 13$	$6 + 8 = 14$

9

13 - 6 = 7	14 - 8 = 6	16 - 7 = 9	15 - 6 = 9
16 - 8 = 8	14 - 7 = 7	15 - 7 = 8	14 - 6 = 8
17 - 9 = 8	18 - 8 = 10	12 - 5 = 7	12 - 8 = 4
11 - 4 = 7	12 - 7 = 5	13 - 5 = 8	14 - 5 = 9
14 - 6 = 8	17 - 8 = 9	15 - 7 = 8	12 - 4 = 8
12 - 6 = 6	13 - 8 = 5	18 - 8 = 10	14 - 5 = 9
16 - 8 = 8	17 - 6 = 11	14 - 6 = 8	12 - 7 = 5
11 - 6 = 5	12 - 3 = 9	11 - 7 = 4	16 - 7 = 9
10 - 5 = 5	11 - 8 = 3	12 - 8 = 4	19 - 7 = 12
19 - 12 = 7	15 - 4 = 11	17 - 8 = 9	13 - 7 = 6

LESSON 9 WORKSHEET B

12 - 5 = 7	13 - 4 = 9	14 - 7 = 7	12 - 6 = 6
15 - 7 = 8	13 - 8 = 5	12 - 7 = 5	11 - 3 = 8
12 - 8 = 4	16 - 8 = 8	12 - 3 = 9	11 - 5 = 6
13 - 5 = 8	11 - 7 = 4	10 - 5 = 5	15 - 6 = 9
16 - 7 = 9	17 - 9 = 8	18 - 9 = 9	14 - 8 = 6
14 - 6 = 8	15 - 8 = 7	14 - 5 = 9	11 - 6 = 5
10 - 5 = 5	11 - 8 = 3	12 - 5 = 7	19 - 10 = 9
7 dollars	7 slices	7 seashells	9 correct answers
April 7th			

LESSON 9 WORKSHEET C

18 - 9 = 9	16 - 7 = 9	12 - 8 = 4	19 - 10 = 9
16 - 5 = 11	17 - 4 = 13	18 - 12 = 6	15 - 8 = 7
14 - 7 = 7	13 - 8 = 5	12 - 7 = 5	18 - 6 = 12
17 - 8 = 9	15 - 7 = 8	16 - 8 = 8	23 - 5 = 18
25 - 8 = 17	14 - 8 = 6	19 - 7 = 12	20 - 7 = 13
8 + 7 = 15	6 + 9 = 15	7 + 6 = 13	4 + 8 = 12
5 + 8 = 13	6 + 6 = 12	7 + 7 = 14	8 + 9 = 17
6 + 5 = 11	8 + 6 = 14	9 + 5 = 14	10 + 7 = 17
8 + 3 = 11	7 + 5 = 12	4 + 7 = 11	9 + 7 = 16
4 + 9 = 13	11 + 6 = 17	9 + 11 = 20	18 + 5 = 23

TEST

45 SECOND TEST NO. 9

16 - 8 = 8	13 - 6 = 7	15 - 8 = 7	17 - 9 = 8
15 - 6 = 9	13 - 5 = 8	15 - 7 = 8	13 - 7 = 6
13 - 8 = 5	11 - 4 = 7	12 - 7 = 5	12 - 8 = 4
14 - 6 = 8	16 - 7 = 9	17 - 8 = 9	13 - 7 = 6

10

27 + 4 = 31	28 + 3 = 31	17 + 4 = 21	18 + 5 = 23
13 + 3 = 16	19 + 2 = 21	6 + 25 = 31	15 + 6 = 21
17 + 7 = 24	9 + 25 = 34	6 + 18 = 24	7 + 37 = 44
9 + 46 = 55	4 + 18 = 22	72 + 3 = 75	18 + 8 = 26
9 + 16 = 25	8 + 12 = 20	8 + 39 = 47	17 + 9 = 26
25 + 7 = 32	82 + 6 = 88	12 + 27 = 39	23 + 8 = 31

33 - 6 = 27	14 - 8 = 6	25 - 7 = 18	52 - 5 = 47
12 - 7 = 5	13 - 8 = 5	18 - 8 = 10	14 - 5 = 9
36 - 8 = 28	17 - 6 = 11	14 - 8 = 6	12 - 6 = 6
21 - 6 = 15	22 - 4 = 18	17 - 7 = 10	16 - 7 = 9
10 - 5 = 5	11 - 8 = 3	32 - 8 = 24	19 - 7 = 12
19 - 12 = 7	55 - 4 = 51	27 - 8 = 19	13 - 6 = 7
27 - 9 = 18	44 - 6 = 38	62 - 8 = 54	25 - 7 = 18

LESSON 10 WORKSHEET B

12 + 5 = 17	15 - 7 = 8	23 + 8 = 31	11 - 3 = 8
20 - 6 = 14	5 + 29 = 34	13 - 7 = 6	8 + 33 = 41
26 + 8 = 34	35 - 7 = 28	38 + 4 = 42	40 - 5 = 35
46 - 9 = 37	52 + 5 = 57	55 - 6 = 49	43 + 8 = 35
7 + 45 = 52	63 - 8 = 55	11 + 57 = 68	36 - 9 = 27
75 - 8 = 67	84 + 9 = 93	19 - 7 = 12	16 + 4 = 20

Continue...

LESSON 10 WORKSHEET B CONTINUED

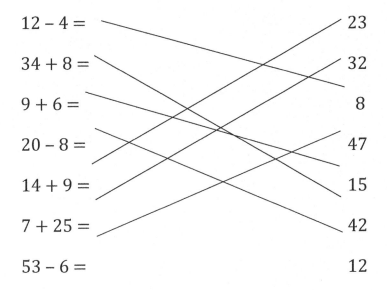

12 − 4 =   23

34 + 8 =   32

9 + 6 =   8

20 − 8 =   47

14 + 9 =   15

7 + 25 =   42

53 − 6 =   12

LESSON 10 WORKSHEET C

32 + 6 = 38	17 + 8 = 25	23 + 9 = 32	15 + 6 = 21
28 + 3 = 31	29 + 7 = 36	8 + 13 = 21	18 + 7 = 25
27 + 5 = 32	5 + 19 = 24	8 + 16 = 24	3 + 41 = 44
7 + 52 = 59	7 + 24 = 31	68 + 3 = 71	33 + 8 = 41
5 + 17 = 22	4 + 29 = 33	1 + 29 = 30	11 + 6 = 17
22 + 9 = 31	68 + 6 = 74	14 + 7 = 21	14 + 8 = 22

24 − 6 = 18	42 − 8 = 34	12 − 7 = 5	38 − 5 = 33
25 − 7 = 18	33 − 8 = 25	27 − 8 = 19	22 − 5 = 17
31 − 8 = 23	23 − 6 = 17	41 − 8 = 33	37 − 6 = 31
51 − 6 = 45	11 − 4 = 7	21 − 7 = 14	14 − 7 = 7
28 − 5 = 23	19 − 8 = 11	29 − 8 = 21	32 − 7 = 25
42 − 12 = 30	60 − 4 = 56	16 − 8 = 8	12 − 6 = 6
31 − 9 = 22	35 − 6 = 49	18 − 8 = 10	23 − 7 = 16

11

20	30	50	70	90	80
50	70	90	80	100	90
60	80	100	100	110	30
100	100	90	90	40	50
110	110	130	120	70	90
60	120	120	140	90	70
130	140	60	110	80	80

70 cents   90 models

LESSON 11 WORKSHEET B

60	110	120	100	70	70
90	60	100	100	100	80
80	140	130	90	110	170
100	120	40	130	90	110
90	130	140	170	100	80

70 minutes   50 people

LESSON 11 WORKSHEET C

1.	30 students	2.	40 minutes	3.	Seventy years old
4.	50 dollars	5.	20 days	6.	42 cans of cat food
7.	20 cans	8.	40 dollars	9.	10 votes
10.	80 years old				

50   100   90   30   20

WORKSHEET 12

90	10	10	10	20	
	10				
60	30	30	60	60	40
10	60	30	20	50	10
80	10	30	50	70	30
50	20	10	40	10	20
60	20	70	50	10	60
70	40	10	40	40	0
50	30	50	10	50	80

20 Cups of juice

LESSON 12 WORKSHEET B

40	30	40	20	10	20
20	10	0	60	40	20
30	10	30	0	20	20

80 – 20 = **60**   90 - 30 = **60**   70 – 40 = **30**
50 - **40** = 10   **80** - 30 = 50   60 - **30** = 30
100 – **30** = 70   40 - **20** = 20   100 – 80 = **20**

70 dollars   40 women

LESSON 12 WORKSHEET C

1.   60 nails   2.   60 dollars   3.   40 chairs

4.   20 teeth   5.   Zero   6.   30 trucks
7.   30 boxes   8.   30 tomatoes   9.   60 pages
10.   Ten dollars

89	74	29	29	25	26
79	69	77	99	69	86
39	39	29	109	29	78
117	28	37	99	39	59
79	33	45	39	59	88
99	89	97	98	79	98
88	49	99	109	39	29

88 apples

LESSON 13 WORKSHEET B

37		28			58
99		67			35
69		40			77

86	49	97	78	27	59
87	96	88	97	48	48

27 spoons		38 books		86

LESSON 13 WORKSHEET C

$38	48 inches	68 boards	28 hours
67 cents	37 people	69 pages	$23

(Bonus Challenging problem) $18.44

WORKSHEET 14

61	65	80	56	55	45
118	31	50	101	42	61
83	33	50	41	67	114
101	91	101	80	82	150
99	126	86	93	135	88
175	121	117	201	187	191

1 driver + 14 kids + 11 kids + 23 kids = **49 people**

LESSON 14 WORKSHEET B

110	40	61	154	100	62
74	46	62	83	71	122
92	71	71	111	161	150
160	124	290	232	214	218
247	150	106	200	210	146

5 coins + 3 coins + 16 coins + 8 coins + 33 coins = 65 coins

LESSON 14 WORKSHEET C

103	101	92	65	74	47
35	105	82	113	54	105
60	102	101	87	112	171
288	83	66	99	150	114
173	137	170	98	110	179

15

1.   250   The 5 is in the ten's column.

2.	One hundred's column	3.	One's column
4.	Ten's column	5.	One hundred's column
6.	One hundred's column	7.	One's column
8.	One's column	9.	Ten's column
10.	One's column	11.	122

12. 564   13. 381   14. 706   15. 100

LESSON 15 WORKSHEET B

645	729	58	920
305	510	813	

729	333	256
612	258	744
925	501	118

2①0   4③5   6⑨1   4⓪7   5①1   3⑦8   2⓪0

15

HUNDRED'S	TEN'S	ONE'S
2	5	3
6	1	4
1	8	5
3	0	5
0	6	3
3	3	4
5	1	0
5	0	5

$50 + 3 + 200 =$

$4 + 10 + 600 =$

$100 + 5 + 80 =$

$5 + 300 =$

$60 + 3 =$

$30 + 4 + 300 =$

$500 + 10 =$

$400 + 90 + 15 =$

If I gave you two $100 bills, six $1 bills and four $10 bills, how much money would I have given you? **$246**

If I gave you eight $1 bills and three $100 bills, how much money would that equal? **$308**

16

11	42	33	23	42	42
31	13	21	31	45	57
46	41	22	24	21	31

22	54	33	40	62	45
52	22	35	10	33	44
23	63	42	52	21	12

She has $63 left.   42 Dolls

LESSON 16 WORKSHEET B

21	17	67
13	21	24
41	24	53
33	40	66

15	12	31	51	40	32

85	57	98	44	86	64
- 72	- 31	-76	- 23	- 56	-22
13	26	22	21	30	44

74	88	97	75	79	19
-43	- 45	-52	-23	- 36	-13
31	43	45	52	43	6

941	555	842	732	543	243
521	432	504	322	411	116
7,021	5,412	4,112	5,023	1,212	2,221

333		222		553
410		475		700
123		402		111

310 more people

17

48	59	48	46	8	9
8	6	28	29	38	8
18	4	18	7	8	43
36	49	39	16	7	16
44	19	18	6	9	18
57	45	35	17	16	19
18	36	7	16	17	9

Teresa has $16 left.　　　　68 puzzle pieces

LESSON 17 WORKSHEET B

8	18	9	12	8	6
27	24	19	23	16	8
45	38	15	18	46	39
17	45	26	18	9	18
32	19	18	39	15	67

57 balls of yarn　　　36 time machine parts

LESSON 17 WORKSHEET C

79	88	45	16	69	89
19	16	48	28	18	18
329	606	729	877	334	664
72	174	283	197	93	177

111 plastic bricks　　　9 dog bones

LESSON 18 WORKSHEET

329	554	748	166	622	368
158	88	292	278	207	584
557	788	319	259	782	736
867	467	575	108	683	665
77	842	583	35	262	585
388	579	639	456	293	341

425 – 88 = 337 comic books

$$\begin{array}{r} {}^{11}\ \ {}^{17} \\ 4\ \not{5}\ \not{7}\ {}^{10} \\ \not{5}\,\not{2}\,\not{8}\,\not{0} \\ -4\ 6\ 9\ 7 \\ \hline \end{array}$$

5 8 3 feet more

LESSON 18 WORKSHEET B

87	181	289	583	129	257
207	306	689	226	868	555
572	348	879	815	486	159
36	574	54	477	182	588
193	259	223	955	315	469

319 wildflowers   146 pastries

LESSON 18 WORKSHEET C

487	464	698	268	677
467	795	858	261	689
2,696	876	409	3,286	6,898

108 cookies   23 problems   38 dollars   206 graduates $33

Review

1.	14	2.	14	3.	16
4.	21	5.	20	6.	24
7.	29	8.	26	9.	32
10.	41	11.	55	12.	91
13.	94	14.	144	15.	129
16.	254	17.	622	18.	450
19.	14,552	20.	1,387	21.	92,438
22.	84 strawberries	23.	809,591 points		

24.	5	25.	4	26.	4
27.	5	28.	15	29.	12
30.	8	31.	22	32.	26
33.	26	34.	24	35.	5

36. 19 pencils   37. 5,779 people

38. 2,625   39. 360   40. 12,049
41. 106,819   42. 7,934   43. 101

44. 26 years   45 38 dollars

CHAPTER 2 TEST

CHAPTER 2 REVIEW TEST

1.	15	2.	14	3.	13
4.	18	5.	19	6.	20
7.	28	8.	27	9.	31
10.	51	11.	53	12.	68
13.	98	14.	99	15.	109

16.	133	17.	101	18.	100

19.	157	20.	260	21.	174
22	2,435	23.	8,308	24.	34,621

25.   a).   758 + 1,543 = 2,301 miles

        b).   The number 3 is in the hundred's column.

26.	4	27.	4	28.	7
29.	8	30.	8	31.	8
32.	22	33.	34	34.	68
35.	20	36.	30	37.	60
38.	511	39.	701	40.	912
41.	818	42.	542	43.	2,187
44.	317	45.	4,385	46.	2,003

47.	9	48.	7	49.	4

50.   2000 – 1687 = 313 more people.

51.   199 + 49 = 248   300 – 248 = 52 dollars

52.   1734 – 1249 = 485 text messages

53.   Maggi's birthday is April 19

CHAPTER 3

WORKSHEET ANSWERS

LearnMathFastBooks.com

LESSON 19 WORKSHEET

10	5	0	4	6	4
20	8	12	9	10	14
3	8	2	7	12	16
6	0	6	14	0	20
1	4	10	0	18	6
8	12	7	8	5	16
0	2	20	14	12	0
18	10	4	8	7	0

Six shoes   10 flowers

LESSON 19 WORKSHEET B

4	3	0	8
5	6	7	14
0	0	12	2
10	16	0	18
0	10	9	12
6	12	16	0
6	8	0	16

Zero   nine   twenty
10 Cookies   Six books   21 students

19

5	2	0	2
2	1	2	1
0	1	2	2
1	4	3	0

16	5	14	0	3	8
0	20	1	18	24	72

6	10	9	0	12	4
21	24	3	18	15	8

4 x 3 = **12**	2 x 4 = **8**	2 x 3 = **6**	2 x 7 = **14**
6 x 2 = **12**	8 x 2 = **16**	3 x 3 = **9**	3 x 6 = **18**
6 x 1 = **6**	2 x 7 = **14**	8 x 0 = **0**	6 x 2 = **12**
3 x 1 = **3**	2 x 2 = **4**	3 x 3 = **9**	2 x 5 = **10**
2 x 9 = **18**	3 x 7 = **21**	3 x 8 = **24**	3 x 6 = **18**
2 x 7 = **14**	2 x 4 = **8**	2 x 5 = **10**	8 x 2 = **16**
0 x 3 = **0**	6 x 2 = **12**	3 x 2 = **6**	7 x 3 = **21**
6 x 3 = **18**	3 x 4 = **12**	4 x 2 = **8**	3 x 5 = **15**
2 x 2 = **4**	4 x 2 = **8**	7 x 2 = **14**	3 x 8 = **24**

3 x 6 = 18 cans of pop.   **3 x 3 = 9 puppies**

LESSON 20 WORKSHEET B

3	6	8	9
10	12	12	0
18	15	7	18
14	4	21	16
24	12	6	15
9	16	9	6
18	21	20	24

2	4	0	2
1	2	5	7
6	8	2	3
2	6	10	4
24 pieces of gum		15 seeds	

20

1.   12 bows
2.   12 people
3.   9 windows
4.   18 cheeseburgers
5.   14 forks
6.   12 wheels
7.   8 horse legs
8. $21
9. $70
10. 24 eggs

TEST

1 MINUTE TEST NO. 10

$2 \times 1 = 2$ $3 \times 3 = 9$ $3 \times 4 = 12$ $2 \times 0 = 0$

$2 \times 2 = 4$ $3 \times 2 = 6$ $3 \times 0 = 0$ $2 \times 8 = 16$

$3 \times 8 = 24$ $3 \times 7 = 21$ $2 \times 7 = 14$ $4 \times 2 = 8$

$5 \times 2 = 10$ $2 \times 6 = 12$ $3 \times 1 = 3$ $5 \times 3 = 15$

$6 \times 3 = 18$ $2 \times 3 = 6$ $7 \times 3 = 21$ $8 \times 3 = 24$

$4 \times 3 = 12$ $8 \times 2 = 16$ $3 \times 5 = 15$ $3 \times 3 = 9$

$3 \times 8 = 24$ $3 \times 7 = 21$ $6 \times 3 = 18$ $3 \times 4 = 12$

LESSON 21 WORKSHEET

8	20	12	6	15	32
21	24	28	24	9	16

3 x **7** = 21	3 x **3** = 9	3 x **8** = 24	3 x **4** = 12
3 x **6** = 18	4 x **8** = 32	8 x **4** = 32	8 x **3** = 24
2 x 3 = **6**	3 x 4 = **12**	1 x 3 = **3**	2 x 7 = **14**
3 x 7 = **21**	8 x 2 = **16**	3 x 3 = **9**	3 x 6 = **18**
4 x 1 = **4**	2 x 4 = **8**	4 x 4 = **16**	4 x 0 = **0**
4 x 5 = **20**	3 x 2 = **6**	8 x 3 = **24**	3 x 5 = **15**
2 x 9 = **18**	3 x 6 = **18**	4 x 8 = **32**	4 x 6 = **24**
4 x 7 = **28**	3 x 4 = **12**	2 x 5 = **10**	8 x 2 = **16**
0 x 3 = **0**	2 x 6 = **12**	4 x 2 = **8**	7 x 3 = **21**
4 x 4 = **16**	5 x 4 = **20**	4 x 1 = **4**	5 x 3 = **15**

20 fingers and toes

LESSON 21 WORKSHEET B

2	2	2	6
4	6	3	2
4	2	5	8
1	6	0	7
6 hours	32 minutes	28 cars	15 windows

Three cans at $2 each =	6
Four bottles at $4 each =	16
Six jars at $3 each =	18
Four bags at $5 each =	20
	$60

21

$$4 \times 3 =$$

$$3 \times 8 =$$

$$3 \times 3 =$$

$$6 \times 3 =$$

$$4 \times 8 =$$

$$7 \times 3 =$$

9

21

12

24

18

32

9	8	16	6	10
14	20	21	4	15
24	12	16	18	12
28	3	20	32	9
18	27	28	12	4
30	15	0	24	32

20 rocks

TEST

30 SECOND TEST NO. 11

$4 \times 4 = 16$	$4 \times 5 = 20$	$3 \times 3 = 9$	$3 \times 6 = 18$
$8 \times 4 = 32$	$8 \times 3 = 24$	$7 \times 3 = 21$	$7 \times 4 = 28$
$6 \times 4 = 24$	$6 \times 3 = 18$	$5 \times 3 = 15$	$4 \times 3 = 12$
$3 \times 2 = 6$	$4 \times 8 = 32$	$4 \times 7 = 28$	$3 \times 8 = 24$

5	10	10	5
15	20	15	20
25	30	30	25
35	40	35	40
45	50	50	45
25	10	20	15

5, **10, 15, 20, 25,** 30, **35, 40,** 45 50

How many nickels?   How much money?

2   10 cents

4   **20** cents

3   **15** cents

5   **25** cents

8   **40** cents

10   **50** cents

2 x 2 = **4**	3 x 3 = **9**	4 x 4 = **16**	5 x 5 = **25**
3 x 4 = **12**	7 x 3 = **21**	6 x 3 = **18**	8 x 3 = **24**
4 x 6 = **24**	8 x 4 = **32**	4 x 5 = **20**	7 x 4 = **28**
5 x 8 = **40**	6 x 5 = **30**	3 x 5 = **15**	5 x 7 = **35**
50 cents	$30	50 pages	24 pieces of candy

7 x 4 = 28 cat shoes

LESSON 22 WORKSHEET B

1 dime + 2 nickels = 20 cents	4 nickels = 20 cents
1 dime + 1 nickel = 15 cents	2 nickels + 1 penny = 11 cents
3 nickels = 15 cents	1 dime + 5 pennies = 15 cents
2 dimes + 2 nickels = 30 cents	5 nickels = 25 cents
1 dime + 3 nickels + 4 pennies = 29 cents	3 dimes = 30 cents

1 x 5 = 5	4 x 5 = 20	5 x 3 = 15	5 x 1 = 5
6 x 5 = 30	3 x 5 = 15	7 x 5 = 35	5 x 4 = 20
5 x 2 = 10	5 x 6 = 30	5 x 8 = 40	2 x 5 = 10
5 x 7 = 35	5 x 5 = 25	5 x 10 = 50	0 x 5 = 0
15 games	35 pieces of cake		

LESSON 22 WORKSHEET C

5 10 **15 20 25 30 35 40 45** 50

2 4 6 8 10 12 14 16 18 20

(4) 9 7 5 (2) (10) (76) 83 (90) 65 (42) 11 55 77 (60) 13 (6) (14)

8 x 5 = 40	8 x 3 = 24	8 x 4 = 32	5 x 6 = 30
$25	32 braids	$35	32 slices
40 gigabytes			

TEST

1 MINUTE TEST NO. 12

3 x 4 = 12	8 x 4 = 32	7 x 5 = 35	6 x 3 = 18
4 x 7 = 28	5 x 4 = 20	2 x 8 = 16	2 x 7 = 14
3 x 3 = 9	5 x 3 = 15	4 x 4 = 16	4 x 6 = 24
5 x 8 = 40	9 x 5 = 45	2 x 6 = 12	2 x 4 = 8
5 x 5 = 25	5 x 1 = 5	2 x 5 = 10	6 x 0 = 0
6 x 5 = 30	1 x 8 = 8	9 x 0 = 0	2 x 3 = 6
3 x 7 = 21	8 x 3 = 24	2 x 2 = 4	3 x 1 = 3
4 x 2 = 8	4 x 1 = 4	1 x 0 = 0	5 x 10 = 50

23

$21 \div 7 = 3$	$24 \div 6 = 4$	$32 \div 8 = 4$	$12 \div 2 = 6$
$9 \div 3 = 3$	$24 \div 3 = 8$	$8 \div 2 = 4$	$28 \div 7 = 4$
$5 \div 1 = 5$	$18 \div 6 = 3$	$16 \div 8 = 2$	$15 \div 3 = 5$
$20 \div 5 = 4$	$10 \div 2 = 5$	$14 \div 7 = 2$	$16 \div 4 = 4$
$4 \div 2 = 2$	$32 \div 4 = 8$	$28 \div 4 = 7$	$24 \div 8 = 3$
$6 \div 3 = 2$	$8 \div 4 = 2$	$12 \div 3 = 4$	$20 \div 4 = 5$

$3 \times 3 = 9$	$2 \times 8 = 16$	$4 \times 6 = 24$	$5 \times 3 = 15$
$2 \times 5 = 10$	$4 \times 5 = 20$	$2 \times 7 = 14$	$4 \times 7 = 28$
$5 \times 1 = 5$	$3 \times 6 = 18$	$7 \times 3 = 21$	$4 \times 3 = 12$
$4 \times 4 = 16$	$2 \times 6 = 12$	$3 \times 8 = 25$	$4 \times 8 = 32$
$4 \times 1 = 4$	$3 \times 0 = 0$	$4 \times 2 = 8$	$3 \times 2 = 6$
$3 \times 4 = 12$	$2 \times 1 = 2$	$2 \times 2 = 4$	$2 \times 0 = 0$

3 cookies

LESSON 23 WORKSHEET B

2	2	5	3	6
18	8	7	3	4
4	4	4	4	5
7	2	8	3	3
5	3	8	9	2
3	2	3	8	5
3	4	7	3	8
24	16	10	8	18
9	12	14	6	15
24	21	20	14	12
32	16	25	0	20

7 cards   8 astronauts per spaceship

LESSON 23 WORKSHEET C

12	6		20	5
16	8		24	8
9	3			

LESSON 24 WORKSHEET

18 = 6 and 3
12 = 4 and 3 or 6 and 2
21 = 7 and 3
32 = 8 and 4 or 16 and 2
24 = 6 and 4 or 8 and 3
9 = 3 and 3
16 = 8 and 2 or 4 and 4
20 = 5 and 4 or 10 and 2
10 = 5 and 2
6 = 2 and 3
4 = 2 and 2
15 = 5 and 3
14 = 7 and 2

3	3	4
3	4	6
3	5	4

$24 \div 8 = 3$	$32 \div 8 = 4$	$21 \div 7 = 3$	$24 \div 6 = 4$
$20 \div 4 = 5$	$15 \div 5 = 3$	$18 \div 3 = 6$	$28 \div 4 = 7$
$28 \div 7 = 4$	$35 \div 5 = 7$	$24 \div 3 = 8$	$24 \div 4 = 6$
$16 \div 4 = 4$	$40 \div 5 = 8$	$18 \div 6 = 3$	$12 \div 4 = 3$

7	5	2
5	4	6
8	7	5

10 = 2 and 5

6 = 3 and 2

14 = 7 and 2   25 = 5 and 5

9 = 3 and 3   8 = 4 and 2

15 = 5 and 3   18 = 6 and 3 or 2 and 9

21 = 3 and 7

16 = 8 and 2, 4 and 4

20 = 4 and 5, 2 and 10

18 = 9 and 2, 6 and 3

12 = 6 and 2, 3 and 4

24 = 8 and 3, 6 and 4, 12 and 2

$24 \div 4 = 6$ $32 \div 4 = 8$ $30 \div 5 = 6$ $28 \div 4 = 7$ $40 \div 5 = 8$

24

24 = 6 x 4   12 = 4 x 3   16 = 4 x 4
    8 x 3   3 x 4   2 x 8
    12 x 2   12 x 1   1 x 16
    24 x 1   2 x 6   8 x 2

20 = 2 x 10   18 = 6 x 3
    4 x 5   2 x 9
    5 x 4   9 x 2
    20 x 1   1 x 18

They are all **EVEN** numbers.

6 x 7 = **42**	6 x 6 = **36**	6 x 3 = **18**	6 x 8 = **48**
6 x 4 = **24**	6 x 5 = **30**	3 x 7 = **21**	3 x 8 = **24**
6 x 2 = **12**	4 x 7 = **28**	8 x 1 = **8**	10 x 2 = **20**
3 x 2 = **6**	8 x 2 = **16**	4 x 8 = **32**	5 x 5 = **25**
2 x 9 = **18**	2 x 7 = **14**	5 x 8 = **40**	3 x 6 = **18**
4 x 6 = **24**	8 x 4 = **32**	6 x 5 = **30**	6 x 2 = **12**
7 x 3 = **21**	7 x 5 = **35**	8 x 3 = **24**	6 x 8 = **48**
4 x 3 = **12**	6 x 6 = **36**	6 x 7 = **42**	3 x 5 = **15**
4 x 4 = **16**	4 x 6 = **24**	8 x 4 = **32**	3 x 8 = **24**
3 x 3 = **9**	3 x 4 = **12**	3 x 6 = **18**	3 x 7 = **21**

36 ÷ 6 = **6**	42 ÷ 6 = **7**	30 ÷ 6 = **5**	24 ÷ 6 = **4**
48 ÷ 6 = **8**	18 ÷ 6 = **3**	6 ÷ 6 = **1**	12 ÷ 6 = **2**

There are 8 Students left the room.

LESSON 25 WORKSHEET B

25	24	6	12	28
16	15	18	18	48
0	6	20	36	21
8	9	24	40	30
42	20	12	16	14
4	48	32	35	42
6	6	5	10	5
5	4	6	7	6
6	3	3	4	8

24 Tickets	42 stickers	6 sunflower seeds

25

36	48	42	35	30	16
15	32	21	24	18	28

7	3	3	6
7	6	6	4
4	7	6	8

4 plants per garden   7 people   48 pages   30 cookies

5 plants per row   3 bottles   8 shopping carts per row

TEST

30 SECOND TEST NO. 13

6 x 6 = 36	6 x 8 = 48	3 x 6 = 18	5 x 6 = 30
5 x 5 = 25	7 x 6 = 42	2 x 6 = 12	4 x 6 = 24
4 x 4 = 16	8 x 4 = 32	3 x 7 = 21	5 x 6 = 30
6 x 1 = 6	8 x 5 = 40	6 x 6 = 36	7 x 6 = 42

7	35	56	21	28
49	0	14	42	56

7	5	7	2
3	8	4	1

18	12	21	56
42	48	56	32
8 pages	6 dollars	6 chocolate chips	

LESSON 26 WORKSHEET B

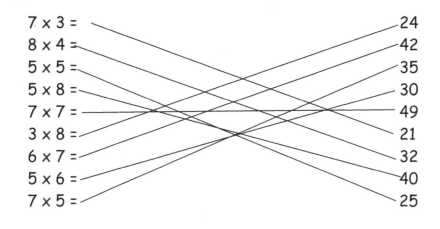

	7 x 3 =		24
8 x 4 =		42
5 x 5 =		35
5 x 8 =		30
7 x 7 =		49
3 x 8 =		21
6 x 7 =		32
5 x 6 =		40
7 x 5 =		25

$20 \div 10 = 2$	$6 \times 5 = 30$	$3 \times 6 = 18$	$4 \div 2 = 2$	$12 \div 6 = 2$
$5 \times 7 = 35$	$16 \div 4 = 4$	$24 \div 4 = 6$	$8 \times 5 = 40$	$9 \times 2 = 18$
$21 \div 3 = 7$	$7 \times 8 = 56$	$8 \times 4 = 32$	$49 \div 7 = 7$	$27 \div 3 = 9$
$5 \times 5 = 25$	$28 \div 7 = 4$	$42 \div 7 = 6$	$6 \times 8 = 48$	$3 \times 7 = 21$
$18 \div 9 = 2$	$7 \times 7 = 49$	$2 \times 10 = 20$	$56 \div 7 = 8$	$32 \div 8 = 4$

$56

26

CROSS-NUMBER PUZZLE

Use numbers to fill in the boxes with the answers to the questions on page 2.

	3	2		2	4				2	4
	0		1	0	3		3	2	4	
	1	0			2	5	6			
2	8			1	5				9	
4		1	2		7		3	0	1	
	5		1	4		4	5		0	
	3	6		2	0	8				4
1	8		2					4	3	0
	1	0	5		2	4		9		
		6	4	5				4	9	
	3	6					1	5	2	
	5		2	7	1		4	8		2
1		1	8		4	2		8	7	1
2	0			7			2	4		

TEST

Answer the following 15 problems in less than 30 seconds. If you can do that, then you are ready for the next lesson.

6	8	7	6	8	7	7
x 6	x 7	x 7	x 7	x 6	x 8	x 6
36	56	49	42	48	56	42

$42 \div 6 = 7$ $56 \div 7 = 8$ $48 \div 6 = 8$ $49 \div 7 = 7$

$36 \div 6 = 6$ $42 \div 7 = 6$ $56 \div 8 = 7$ $48 \div 8 = 6$

LESSON 27 WORKSHEET

8	40	56	24	32
64	0	16	48	64

8	3	6	8
4	8	4	7

32	21	24	56
28	40	16	48

8 students $48   5 hours

LESSON 27 WORKSHEET B

35	8	40	7
8	0	4	64
56	6	48	8
5	24	8	16
18	7	30	6

24 = 3 and 8 or 6 and 4   40 = 8 and 5 or 10 and 4   21 = 7 and 3

16 = 8 and 2 or 4 and 4   30 = 6 and 5 or 10 and 3   32 = 8 and 4 or 16 and 2

56 = 8 and 7, 2 and 28 or 14 and 4   42 = 6 and 7   64 = 8 and 8

28 = 7 and 4 or 2 and 14   48 = 6 and 8   36 = 6 and 6

35 = 7 and 5   8 = 4 and 2   18 = 6 and 3 or 9 and 2

8 packs of bricks $56

27

8	6	3	7	5	4
5	3	6	8	4	7
3	5	4	8	7	6
18	24	30	36	42	48
21	28	35	42	49	56
24	32	40	48	56	64

TEST

30 SECOND TEST NO. 15

Are you ready? You've got 30 seconds to try to answer all these problems aloud. On your mark, get set, go!

8 x 8 = 64	7 x 8 = 56	6 x 6 = 36	7 x 7 = 49
6 x 8 = 48	4 x 8 = 32	5 x 8 = 40	3 x 8 = 24
4 x 6 = 24	7 x 3 = 21	4 x 3 = 12	8 x 2 = 16
3 x 3 = 9	4 x 5 = 20	6 x 3 = 18	8 x 8 = 64

LESSON 28 WORKSHEET

9	45	63	27	36
72	0	18	54	81

6	8	9	5
4	7	2	3

90	81	27	63
36	45	72	54

3	2	6	4
1	8	7	5
7	8	9	1
5	2	4	10

LESSON 28 WORKSHEET B

9	32	27	20
21	18	72	54
36	56	45	64
81	0	63	48

2	6	9	8
8	4	8	6
9	7	7	6
7	9	5	7

7	2	5	1
4	8	6	3
8	5	6	7
4	9	6	7

36 songs

1. $27 2. 18 points 3. 54 windows
4. 63 golf balls 5. 45 birthday cards 6. 36 pages
7. 72 people 8. 81 copies

7   8   4   6   2

TEST

It is time for another 30 second test. If you can correctly answer these 16 problems aloud in 30 seconds, you are ready for the next lesson.

9 x 6 = 54   9 x 4 = 36   9 x 7 = 63   9 x 3 = 27

9 x 8 = 72   9 x 5 = 45   9 x 2 = 18   9 x 9 = 81

9 x 0 = 0   8 x 8 = 64   6 x 8 = 48   4 x 8 = 32

4 x 9 = 36   3 x 9 = 27   8 x 9 = 72   9 x 1 = 9

LESSON 29 WORKSHEET

10 x 7 = **70**	10 x 6 = **60**	100 x 3 = **300**	10 x 8 = **80**
10 x 4 = **40**	100 x 5 = **500**	9 x 10 = **90**	1 x 10 = **10**
10 x 2 = **20**	4 x 100 = **400**	5 x 10 = **50**	10 x 0 = **0**
3 x 10 = **30**	10 x 10 = **100**	1 x 100 = **100**	100 x 2 = **200**
2 x 9 = **18**	2 x 7 = **14**	5 x 10 = **50**	3 x 6 = **18**
4 x 9 = **36**	8 x 7 = **56**	6 x 5 = **30**	6 x 8 = **48**
7 x 3 = **21**	7 x 5 = **35**	8 x 3 = **24**	7 x 8 = **56**
4 x 3 = **12**	6 x 6 = **36**	6 x 7 = **42**	8 x 8 = **64**
7 x 7 = **49**	10 x 6 = **60**	8 x 100 = **800**	4 x 8 = **32**
3 x 9 = **27**	9 x 4 = **36**	4 x 6 = **24**	3 x 7 = **21**
4 x 7 = **28**	100 x 5 = **500**	5 x 5 = **25**	8 x 5 = **40**
9 x 2 = **18**	4 x 4 = **16**	9 x 3 = **27**	9 x 8 = **72**
8 x 6 = **48**	6 x 6 = **36**	6 x 7 = **42**	7 x 7 = **49**

LESSON 29 WORKSHEET B

14	70	24	72	25
30	30	45	80	300
48	200	49	20	36
50	28	18	40	63
32	100	9	10	36
15	81	210	56	60
14	70	24	72	25
50,000	54	480,000	40	
35	90	20	42	10
0	10	70	12	20,000
27	7,000	10,000	9,000	
5	10	6	10	
3	6	6	9	
10	7	7	20	450 chocolate chips

29

10	100	350
20	200	250
30	300	900
40	400	4,000
50	500	8,100
60	600	4,200
70	700	640
80	800	560
90	900	4,800
100	1,000	6,300

100 stars   900 pounds   10 students   9,000 votes

TEST

30 SECOND TEST NO. 17

$4 \times 100 = 400$ $6 \times 60 = 360$ $7 \times 70 = 490$ $3 \times 30 = 90$

$80 \times 4 = 320$ $3 \times 10 = 30$ $60 \times 10 = 600$ $80 \times 8 = 640$

$30 \times 7 = 210$ $8 \times 10 = 80$ $9 \times 60 = 540$ $10 \times 10 = 100$

$6 \times 80 = 480$ $30 \times 10 = 300$ $9 \times 30 = 270$ $10 \times 5 = 50$

LESSON 30 WORKSHEET

10 × 11 = **110**	7 × 11 = **77**	11 × 6 = **66**	11 × 3 = **33**
8 × 11 = **88**	11 × 4 = **44**	11 × 5 = **55**	11 × 100 =**1,100**
11 × 1 = **11**	2 × 11 = **22**	9 × 11 = **99**	11 × 11 = **121**
11 × 13 = **143**	16 × 11 = **176**	11 × 14 = **154**	11 × 80 = **880**
11 × 17 = **187**	11 × 18 = **198**	70 × 11 = **770**	10 × 11 = **110**
9 × 90 = **810**	11 × 6 = **66**	5 × 11 = **55**	2 × 11 = **22**
10 × 11 = **110**	11 × 11 = **121**	11 × 60 = **660**	70 × 11 = **770**
60 × 11 = **660**	40 × 11 = **440**	300 × 11 = **3,300**	25 × 11 = **275**
18 × 110 = **1,980**	110 × 6 = **660**	20 × 11 = **220**	100 × 11 = **1,100**
1000 × 11=**11,000**	7 × 110 = **770**	12 × 10 = **120**	62 × 10 = **620**
80 × 6 = **480**	7 × 70 = **490**	70 × 6 = **420**	8 × 80 = **640**
9 × 90 = **810**	30 × 8 = **240**	7 × 30 = **210**	80 × 4 = **320**

LESSON 30 WORKSHEET B

11 × 4 = 44	20 × 3 = 60	8 × 11 = 88	40 × 10 = 400
10 × 10 = 100	11 × 11 = 121	20 × 70 = 1,400	11 × 12 = 132
11 × 6 = 66	15 × 11 = 165	11 × 10 = 110	300 × 40 = 12,000
18 × 11 = 198	11 × 3 = 33	14 × 11 = 154	11 × 13 = 143
90 × 90 = 8,100	16 × 11 = 176	50 × 11 = 550	72 × 10 = 720
11 × 100 = 1,100	70 × 60 = 4,200	10 × 110 = 1,110	11 × 14 = 154
12 × 11 = 132	11 × 140 = 1,540	70 × 11 = 770	150 × 11 = 1,650
80 × 6 = 480	110 × 15 = 1,650	90 × 4 = 360	7 × 11 = 77
110 × 160 = 17,600	13 × 11 = 143	60 × 90 = 5,400	11 × 2 = 22
720 ÷ 90 = 8	165 ÷ 11 = 15	240 ÷ 6 = 40	1050 ÷ 10 = 105
198 ÷ 11 = 18	270 ÷ 9 = 30	500 ÷ 50 = 10	110 ÷ 11 = 10
810 ÷ 9 = 90	360 ÷ 40 = 9	132 ÷ 11 = 12	154 ÷ 11 = 14
180 ÷ 30 = 6	770 ÷ 11 = 70	5830 ÷ 10 = 583	99 ÷ 9 = 11

6 apiaries

1.	900 pounds	2.	10 pounds	3.	$1,170
4.	12 people	5.	$198	6.	11 frogs
7.	$154	8.	$198	9.	11 stacks
10.	11 people				

TEST

30 SECOND TEST NO. 18

Can you correctly answer these 24 problems aloud in less than 30 seconds? This test has more problems because it is so easy. Good luck!

9	10	11	9	10	9
x 5	x 7	x 6	x 3	x 4	x 8
45	**70**	**66**	**27**	**40**	**72**

11	10	9	10	9	11
x 9	x 5	x 4	x 3	x 9	x 2
99	**50**	**36**	**30**	**81**	**22**

10	11	9	11	10	9
x 2	x 4	x 3	x 8	x 9	x 0
20	**44**	**27**	**88**	**90**	**0**

9	10	11	10	11	11
x 1	x 4	x 5	x 7	x 10	x 7
9	**40**	**55**	**70**	**110**	**77**

LESSON 31 WORKSHEET

36	40	50	66	42	30
32	52	45	36	80	84
187	70	65	99	26	48
72	56	75	81	85	60

$54 \div 6 = 9$ $42 \div 6 = 7$ $72 \div 8 = 9$ $56 \div 7 = 8$

$35 \div 5 = 7$ $49 \div 7 = 7$ $48 \div 6 = 8$ $18 \div 3 = 6$

$36 \div 6 = 6$ $63 \div 9 = 7$ $55 \div 11 = 5$ $100 \div 10 = 10$

$81 \div 9 = 9$ $45 \div 5 = 9$ $42 \div 7 = 6$ $56 \div 8 = 7$

$40 \div 8 = 5$ $12 \div 4 = 3$ $32 \div 4 = 8$ $28 \div 4 = 7$

$21 \div 3 = 7$ $30 \div 6 = 5$ $64 \div 8 = 8$ $63 \div 7 = 9$

$25 \div 5 = 5$ $27 \div 3 = 9$ $110 \div 10 = 11$ $48 \div 8 = 6$

LESSON 31 WORKSHEET B

$12 \times 2 = 24$ $12 \times 6 = 72$ $10 \times 3 = 30$ $11 \times 7 = 77$

$12 \times 4 = 48$ $10 \times 13 = 130$ $14 \times 2 = 28$ $12 \times 5 = 60$

108	24	84	60	120	132	36
45	70	110	30	48	390	72
39	165	140	84	26	84	56

12	10	6	8
7	11	6	9
4	8	7	9

8	5	23	9
4	6	7	50

21 shoes

1. 4 packs
2. 42 dinner rolls
3. 1,700 bricks
4. 25 customers
5. 200 pounds per day
6. 12 outlets
7. 100 Senators
8. $144

LESSON 32 WORKSHEET

68	84	105	186	75	112
108	133	128	46	140	140
264	308	230	180	144	104
96	203	104	143	243	102
80	234	275	280	280	434
57	448	396	178	616	125
693	352	96	324	392	385
516	651	348	117	240	117

304 pencils

LESSON 32 WORKSHEET B

75	186	105	140	272	440
160	126	414	342	495	216
504	801	81	624	96	183
492	539	65	301	64	680
297	126	128	152	145	300
637	105	180	130	252	448
448	48	256	234	363	891

104 stripes   270 minutes

LESSON 32 WORKSHEET C

2,834	6,109	165	774	194
7,077	587	8,596	47	25
96	140	99	80	4,200
96	144	546	855	396

$100 \div 10 = 10$ $56 \div 8 = 7$ $72 \div 8 = 9$ $120 \div 12 = 10$

$18 \div 6 = 3$ $64 \div 8 = 8$ $77 \div 7 = 11$ $84 \div 12 = 7$

4 girls x 10 potholders = 40 potholders. $40 \div 2 = 20$ **20 sets of two potholders**

16×10 *fingernails* = 160 *fingernails*   160 − 1 *thumb* = 159 *fingernails*

33

484	2912	2568	2106	2145
960	4765	3564	656	1240
6104	6510	4176	2430	928
4368	3437	1132	860	8181
2214	3724	1281	5646	5640
4326	1317	766	540	4725
3948	3000	558	6902	2295
1572	4744	908	6309	2140

LESSON 33 WORKSHEET B

960	666	4,488	644	4.077
6,202	520	2,032	1,454	5,532
1,190	504	4,075	2,322	4,848
1,288	2,538	4,386	2,415	6,849
1,496	3,685	7,560	7,263	420
2,872	1,224	1,660	6,170	6,741
5,526	3,032	4,104	2,925	1,245
49,098	910	5,382	2,744	27,270

2,304 copies   1485 flat sticks

LESSON 33 WORKSHEET C

1. $2,832
2. $2,856
3. $201
4. $861
5. 3,200 coins
6. 3,672 megabytes
7. 490 books
8. $4,930
9. 320 questions
10. 900 seconds

LESSON 34 WORKSHEET

5	8	6	6	6	7
6	7	5	7	3	9
3	6	8	7	3	4
4	3	4	8	3	5
6	2	6	6	5	4
5	5	6	8	9	8
6	3	4	3	3	1
2	9	5	4	4	3

$40 \div 8 = 5$ **5 stacks of cones**

LESSON 34 WORKSHEET B

3	3	8	12	7	5
10	3	9	11	8	5
7	9	6	8	8	7
6	3	7	6	8	3
4	4	7	7	1	9
3	5	4	5	6	10
8	6	3	5	4	7
12	10	7	7	2	9

30 notes   72 kids

1. Each circle should contain eight dollar signs, for example:

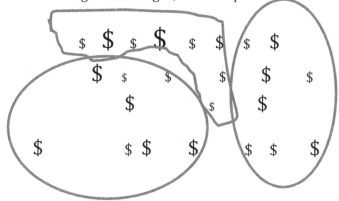

2. $20 ÷ 4 *tickets* = $5 *per ticket*

3.   7 *dogs* × 5 *puppies* = 35 *puppies*   35 *puppies* + 7 *dogs* = 42 *dogs*

4. $400 ÷ 4 *students* = $100 *per*

5.   12 *eggs* ÷ 3 = 4   *You can serve 4 people*

6.   36 *students* ÷ 4 *teams* = 9 *students per team*

7.   45 *signs* ÷ 5 *people* = 9 *signs per person*

8. $72 ÷ 8 = 9$ 9. $42 ÷ 6 = 7$ 10. $48 ÷ 8 = 6$ 11. $49 ÷ 7 = 7$

12.   4   13.   5   14.   9   15.   9

35

```
    32           33           81           71
5) 160       8) 264       6) 486       9) 639
   15           24           48           63
   10           24           06           09
   10           24            6            9
    0            0            0            0


    55           62           98           84
9) 495       7) 434       3) 294       7) 588
   45           42           27           56
   45           14           24           28
   45           14           24           28
    0            0            0            0


   265          420          431          564
8) 2120      3) 1260      9) 3879      3) 1692
   16           12           36           15
   52           06           27           19
   48            6           27           18
   40           00           09           12
   40                         9           12


   724          372          527          691
4) 2896      7) 2604      4) 2108      3) 2073
   28           21           20           18
   09           50           10           27
    8           49            8           27
   16           14           28           03
   16           14           28            3
```

$930 each

75

35

```
     25              29              93              87
6)150           4)116           7)651           9)783
  12              8               63              72
  30              36              21              63
  30              36              21              63
   0               0               0               0
```

```
     77             124             231             360
5)385           8)992           3)693           2)720
  35              8               6               6
  35              19              09              12
  35              16              9               12
   0              32              03               0
                  32              3
                   0               0
```

```
    357             749             816             444
4)1428          6)4494          2)1632          8)3552
  12              42              16              32
  22              29              03              35
  20              24              2               32
  28              54              12              32
  28              54              12              32
   0               0               0               0
```

```
    399             552             617             987
9)3591          7)3864          5)3085          3)2961
  27              35              30              27
  89              36              08              26
  81              35              5               24
  81              14              35              21
  81              14              35              21
   0               0               0               0  Continued...
```

Grandma put 2844 pictures evenly into 9 photo albums. How many pictures are in each photo album? **316 pictures**

There are 6503 grains of rice in a cup. It is poured evenly into 7 smaller cups. How many grains of rice are in each smaller cup? **929 grains of rice**

LESSON 35 WORKSHEET C

1.   18 baskets

2. $25 per hour

3.   700 pillows in each truck

4.   1,200 feet

5.   200 pounds

6. $4,000 per month

1. The 0 is in the one's column
2. **Ten thousand's column**
3. **Hundred's column**
4. **Thousand's column**
5. **Million's column**
6. **Ten's column**
7. **Hundred thousand's column**
8. **Ten billion's column**
9. **Ten Million's column**
10. **One's column**

* Seven hundred twenty-three thousand, four hundred two. 723,402

11. **811,300,512**
12. **5,617**
13. **31,478**
14. **500,000,000**
15. **614,050**
16. **9,000,000**
17. **37,110,042**

LESSON 36 WORKSHEET B

1. The zero is in the ten's column
2. Thousand's column
3. Ten thousand's column
4. Ten Million's column
5. Hundred thousand's column
6. Billion's column

1. 552,384
2. 43,033,199
3. 625,000,000,013
4. 123,456,789
5. 91,809,200

6. Fifty thousand, one hundred fifteen
7. Ten million, three hundred eleven thousand, four hundred ninety-nine
8. Three billion, five hundred sixteen million, seven thousand, one hundred twenty-three

Hundred Billion's	Hundred Million's	Hundred Thousand's	Hundred's

2. Six zeros

3. Six zeros

4. Seven digits

5. 999,999

6. 100,000

7. 600,004

8. 16,000,012,000,000

9. 404,014

10. 56,000,004,784,702

$$\frac{-\quad 12,219,004}{55,999,992,565,698}$$

11.
$$\begin{array}{r} 2,015 \\ 3\overline{)6,045} \\ \underline{6} \\ 004 \\ \underline{3} \\ 15 \\ \underline{15} \\ 0 \end{array}$$

12. 17,000,936,513

$$\frac{\times\ 8}{136,007,492,104}$$

13.
$$\begin{array}{r} 156,951,846 \\ 6\overline{)941,711,076} \\ \underline{6} \\ 34 \\ \underline{30} \\ 41 \\ \underline{36} \\ 57 \\ \underline{54} \\ 31 \\ \underline{30} \\ 11 \\ \underline{6} \\ 50 \\ \underline{48} \\ 27 \\ \underline{24} \\ 36 - 36 = 0 \end{array}$$

238	478	283	182	900
x 13	x 90	x 24	x 75	x 50
714	000	1,132	910	000
2380	43,020	5,660	12,740	45,000
3,094	43,020	6,792	13,650	45,000

262	521	389	941	775
x 79	x 17	x 66	x 12	x 98
2,358	3,647	2,334	1,882	6,200
18,340	5,210	23,340	9,410	69,750
20,698	8,857	25,674	11,292	75,950

721	460	654	108	525
x 36	x 23	x 10	x 103	x 439
4,326	1,380	000	324	4,725
21,630	9,200	6,540	0000	15,750
25,956	10,580	6,540	10,800	210,000
			11,124	230,475

987	375	923	986	765
x 104	x 228	x 612	x 457	x 193
3,948	3,000	1,846	6,902	2,295
0,000	7,500	9,230	49,300	68,850
98,700	75,000	553,800	394,400	76,500
102,648	85,500	564,876	450,602	147,645

567	593	454	701	428
x 907	x 328	x 231	x 259	x 103
3,969	4,744	454	6,309	1,284
0,000	11,860	13,620	35,050	0,000
510,300	177,900	90,800	140,200	42,800
514,269	194,504	104,874	181,559	44,084

37

```
   275          316          445          268          589
 x  21        x  32        x  24        x  43        x  52
   275          632         1780          804         1178
 5500         9480         8900        10,720        29450
 5775        10,112       10,680       11,524        30,628


   190          422          353          746          876
 x  67        x  39        x  45        x  74        x  49
  1330         3798         1765         2984         7884
11400        12660        14120        52220        35040
12,730       16,458       15,885       55,204        42,924


   692          571          606          225          980
 x  55        x  85        x  18        x  63        x  98
  3460         2855         4848          675         7840
34600        46680         6060        13500        88200
38,060       49,535       10,908       14,175        96,040


   363          793          564          921          834
 x  36        x  47        x  96        x  27        x  65
  2178         5551         3384         6447         4170
10890        31720        50760        18420        50040
13,068       37,271       54,144       24,867        54,210


  2,895         338        2,767        8,765       20,846
 x  407       x  965       x  174       x  543       x  378
 20265         1690        11068        26295        166768
 00000        20280       193690       350600       1459220
1158000      304200       276700      4382500       6253800
1,178,265    326,170      481,458     4,759,395     7,879,788


  $295
 x   35 students
  1475
  8850
$10,325
```

```
    6,938        72,106         540,596          320,651
   x  67        x   23         x  495           x 871
   48,566       216,318       2,702,980         320,651
  416,280     1,442,120       48,653,640       22,445,570
  464,946     1,658,338      216,238,400      256,520,800
                             267,595,030      289,287,021
```

| 464,846 | 1,658,438 | 267,595,020 | 279,287,021 |

Solve the first problem, below, and then put that answer in the box above the next problem. Continue solving the problems and moving your answers to the next box.

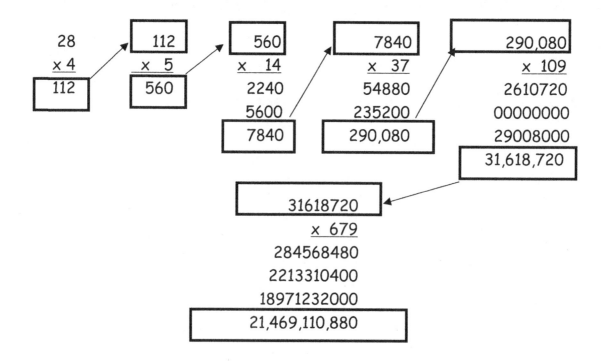

```
   28        112         560          7840          290,080
   x 4       x  5       x   14       x   37        x  109
   112       560        2240         54880         2610720
                        5600        235200         00000000
             [7840]     [7840]      [290,080]      29008000
                                                   31,618,720
```

```
        31618720
        x  679
        284568480
       2213310400
      18971232000
     21,469,110,880
```

*	103	<	104
1.	10.1	>	10.0
2.	.70	>	.07
3.	1.09	>	.09
4.	33,987.5	<	34,092.3
5.	.006	<	.06
6.	17.559	<	17.599
7.	4.709	<	4.719
8.	15.999	>	5.122
9.	.0543	<	.1543
10.	701,945,046.3	<	701,945,146.3

11. Name this math symbol: > **Greater Than**

12. Name this math symbol: < **Less Than**

LESSON 38 WORKSHEET B

*	20	<	20.5
1.	63.63	>	63.36
2.	15.21	>	15.021
3.	2,821.44	<	2,913.25
4.	80.90	>	80.09
5.	.088888874	<	.5555559996
6.	29.2766583	<	29.2766983
7.	50.125	>	50.1125
8.	1.99	<	2
9.	210.1	>	210.01
10.	501,415,853,497.123	<	501,416,853,497.123

Tommy 3 x .25 = .75 8 x .10 = .80 3 x .05 = .15 12 x .01 = .12
.75 + .8 + .15 + .12 = $1.82

Timmy: 4 x .25 = 1 5 x .1 = .5 6 x .05 = .30 14 x .01 = .14
1 + .5 + .30 + .14 = $1.94

Tommy < Timmy

1. $10,000 < $100,000
2. 152 Cats < 172 Cats
3. 126,934 > 126,924
4. 722 = 722
5. 95,000 < 100,000
6. 4,444 < 22,222
7. 5 > 0
8. 1,000,000 = 1,000,000
9. 10 pizzas > 2 slices of pizza
10. 500 pounds of spaghetti is < 800 pounds of macaroni and cheese.

11. 400×20 _____ 60×60	8,000 > 3,600
12. $700 \div 10$ _____ 35×2	70 = 70
13. $936 \div 3$ _____ $872 \div 4$	312 > 218
14. $252 \div 9$ _____ $850 \div 17$	28 < 50

.15	1.684	8.18	13.1	4.97
.232	9.5	11.2	9.18	17.1
86.5	30.2	26.25	9.25	5.132

2.4	.261	154.607	2.8	19.2
.050	.86	2.0	.574	8.6

$6.58 + 12 = 18.58$ $4.5 + .005 = 4.505$ $17.5 + 18.4 = 35.9$ $1.97 + .82 = 2.79$

$.07 + .7 = .77$ $58 + .02 = 58.02$ $12.45 - 3.2 = 9.25$ $17.3 - .089 = 17.211$

LESSON 39 WORKSHEET B

21.0	1.14	.003	24.44	6.5526
27.42	11.322	105.49	10.97	128.4
.011	24.98	18.102	42.65	557.1346

15.9	.999	.657	4.25	72.00
.0607	15.33	.999	41.76	4.19

$3.19 + 4.125 = 7.315$ $8 - 6.24 = 1.76$ $28.21 + 58.718 = 86.928$

$.0155 - .00421 = .01129$ $2.033 + .593 = 2.626$ $97.2 - 50.34 = 46.86$

$140.5 + 113.096 = 253.596$ $1,432.058 - 395 = 1037.058$

$1.0456 + 415.8 = 416.8456$

18.097 + .018 = 18.115   54.09 − 23.99 = 30.10   1,735.008 − 1,342.84 = 392.168

640 + 2.093 = 642.093   .0849 − .0036 = .0813

9,872,092.09 + 642.1 = 9,871,449.99   .076 + 2,964,040 = 2,964,040.076

79,631 − .0089 = 79,630.9911   .9107 − .0628 = .8479

73.45	987.22	1.23	19.550
6.55	− 54.67	4.37	− 18.033
+ 15.00	$932.55	+ 2.00	1.517 *inches*
$95.00		$7.60	

1,200.00	$2.67 15.922	
− 198.43	− 0.40	− 15.768
$1,001.57	$2.27	.154 *pounds*

19.7	2.08	2.7	35.1	5.4
x .4	x 4.2	x .8	x 2.2	x .7
7.88	416	**2.16**	702	**3.78**
	8320		7020	
	8.736		**77.22**	

4.4	6.4	9.5	.42	.897
x.25	x 2.8	x 5.7	x .3	x .2
220	512	665	**.126**	**.1794**
880	1280	4750		
1.100	**17.92**	**54.15**		

4.4	.36	.777	.32	.006
x .11	x .7	x .01	x .5	x .03
44	**.252**	777	**.160**	018
440		0000		0000
.484		**.00777**		**.00018**

8.7	.082	8.30	1.2	7.00
x .63	x .05	x .45	x .7	x .5
261	**.00410**	4150	**.84**	**3.500**
5220		33200		
5.481		**3.7350**		

6.2	1.01	.379	.103	50.1
x 7.9	x .17	x .06	x 1.2	x .7
558	707	**.02274**	206	**35.07**
4340	1010		1030	
48.98	**.1717**		**.1236**	

Continued...

```
   0.4          20.4          .068          1.42           2.5
  x .3         x  10        x 7.4         x .77          x .9
   .12          0000          272           994          2.25
               2040         4760          9940
              204.0        .5032        1.0934


   .97           5.9          2.35          .011           6.5
  x .01         x .8        x .72         x .55          x .7
 .0097          4.72          470           055          4.55
                            16450          550
                           1.6920        .00605


  7.07          5.93           .54          78.1          .462
  x .07        x .22         x.33         x .52         x.348
 .4949          1186           162          1562          3696
  0000         11860          1620         39050         18480
              1.3046         .1782        40.612        138600
                                                       .160776
```

3.16	81.5	15.6	7.3	6.06
× .4	× 3.1	× .83	× 3.3	× 18
1.264	815	468	219	4848
	~~24450~~	~~12480~~	~~2190~~	~~6060~~
	252.65	12.948	24.09	109.08

28	.992	42.9	12	100
× 2.5	× 7	× 6.25	× 1.5	× 3.25
140	6.944	2145	60	500
_____ 560		8580	_____ 120	2000
70.0		257400	18.0	30000
		268.125		325.00

5.405	17.89	1.56	16.3	.142
× 2	× 21	× 1.5	× 20	× 3.5
10.810	1789	780	000	710
	35780	1560	3260	4260
	375.69	**2.340**	**326.0**	**.4970**

90	2.027	8.54	.853	7.14
× 7.3	× 45.9	× 6.5	× 1.2	× 2.76
270	18243	4270	1706	4284
6300	101350	51240	8530	49980
657.0	810800	**55.510**	**1.0236**	142800
	93.0393			**19.7064**

3.14	12	44.8	.125	59.7
× 5.3	× .3	× 1.96	× 7	× 5
942	**3.6**	2688	**.875**	**298.5**
15700		40320		
16.642		44800		
		87.808		

40

1. 14.25 x 3 = 42.75 minutes   2. 42.85 x 80 = $3,428

3. 3.43 x 7 = 24.01 pounds   4. $2.37 x 11 = $26.07

5. .43 tall

$$
\begin{array}{cccccc}
4.67 & 23.479 & .0092 & 754.09 & 32.109 & 7.064 \\
\underline{\times\ 3.2} & \underline{\times\ .098} & \underline{\times\ 55} & \underline{\times\ 2.3} & \underline{\times\ 4.86} & \underline{\times\ .76} \\
934 & 187832 & 0460 & 226227 & 192654 & 42384 \\
\underline{14010} & \underline{2113110} & \underline{04600} & \underline{1508180} & 2568720 & \underline{494480} \\
14.944 & 2.300942 & .5060 & 1734.407 & 12843600 & \mathbf{5.36864}
\end{array}
$$

156.04974

$$
\begin{array}{cccccc}
.98 & 5.397 & 7.0 & .508 & 729.64 & 854,021 \\
\underline{\times\ .36} & \underline{\times\ .31} & \underline{\times\ .27} & \underline{\times\ .06} & \underline{\times\ 27.6} & \underline{\times\ .007} \\
588 & 5397 & 490 & 3048 & 437784 & 5978147 \\
\underline{2940} & \underline{161910} & \underline{1400} & \underline{0000} & 5107480 & \underline{000000} \\
.3528 & 1.67307 & 1.890 & .03048 & 14592800 & \mathbf{5978.147}
\end{array}
$$

20138.064

```
      18 R4              35 R3              94 R2              172 R1
  7) 130            7) 248             4) 378             3) 517
     7                 21                 36                 3
    60                 38                 18                21
    56                 35                 16                21
     4                  3                  2                07
                                                             6
                                                             1


     127 R6             89 R2             189 R1             97 R3
  7) 895            5) 447             3) 568             6) 585
     7                 40                 3                 54
    19                 47                26                 45
    14                 45                24                 42
    55                  2                28                  3
    49                                   27
                                          1


    3384 R1            156 R2             427 R7             349 R3
  2) 6769           8) 1250            9) 3850            4) 1399
     6                  8                 36                12
    07                 45                 25                19
     6                 40                 18                16
    16                 50                 70                39
    16                 48                 63                36
    09                  2                  7                 3
     8


    1218 R6           1243 R1             287 R1            1231 R5
  8) 9750           2) 2487            5) 1436            6) 7391
     8                  2                 10                 6
    17                 04                 43                13
    16                  4                 40                12
    15                 08                 36                19
     8                  8                 35                18
    70                 07                  1                11
    64                  6                                    6
     6                  1                                    5
```

```
     45 R 2          18 R 4          35 R 7          24 R 6
3) 137          6) 112          10) 357          8) 198
   12              6               30              16
   17             52               57              38
   15             48               50              32
    2              4                7               6
```

```
     52 R 2          85 R 5          93 R 1          66 R 5
4) 210          7) 600          2) 187          9) 599
   20             56               18              54
   10             40               07              59
    8             35                6              54
    2              5                1               5
```

```
    125 R 1         234 R 3         385 R 3          897
5) 626          8) 1875         6) 2313         4) 3588
    5             16               18              32
   12             27               51              38
   10             24               48              36
   26             35               33              28
   25             32               30              28
    1              3                3               0
```

Continue...

41

```
   442 R 1          829 R 7          727 R 1          1234 R5
7) 3095          9) 7468          3) 2182          10) 12345
   28               72               21               10
   29               26               08               23
   28               18                6               20
   15               88               22               34
   14               81               21               30
    1                7                1               45
                                                      40
                                                       5
```

There are 8 art supplies left over.

LESSON 41 WORKSHEET C

1. $112 \div 10 = 11\,R2$ There will be 2 sheets left over.

2. $\$5000 \div 6 = \$833$ Each kid should receive $833. There are $2 left over.

   ALTERNATE ANSWER: $833.33 with two cents left over.

3. $1930 \div 150 = 12\,r\,130$ 13 *Shelves are needed.*

4.   How much is 423 plus 391?   814

   Subtract 607 from your answer.   207

   Multiply that answer by 14.   2,898

   Divide that answer by 5   579

   How much is the remainder?   3

   Multiply that number by 10,000 in your mind.   30,000

LESSON 42 WORKSHEET

$102\frac{2}{3}$
$3\overline{)308}$

$100\frac{3}{4}$
$4\overline{)403}$

$76\frac{2}{5}$
$5\overline{)382}$

$96\frac{4}{6}$
$6\overline{)580}$

$122\frac{2}{7}$
$7\overline{)856}$

$93\frac{3}{8}$
$8\overline{)747}$

$88\frac{6}{9}$
$9\overline{)798}$

$129\frac{1}{2}$
$2\overline{)259}$

$1297\frac{4}{5}$
$5\overline{)6489}$

$311\frac{3}{4}$
$4\overline{)1247}$

$1246\frac{2}{3}$
$3\overline{)3740}$

$672\frac{1}{2}$
$2\overline{)1345}$

$1585\frac{2}{6}$
$6\overline{)9512}$

$412\frac{3}{7}$
$7\overline{)2887}$

$183\frac{2}{8}$
$8\overline{)1466}$

$923\frac{4}{9}$
$9\overline{)8311}$

LESSON 42 WORKSHEET B

$92\frac{3}{5}$
$5\overline{)463}$

$74\frac{2}{3}$
$3\overline{)224}$

$421\frac{1}{2}$
$2\overline{)843}$

$118\frac{5}{6}$
$6\overline{)713}$

$356\frac{2}{4}$
$4\overline{)1426}$

$239\frac{6}{9}$
$9\overline{)2157}$

$483\frac{4}{7}$
$7\overline{)3385}$

$58\frac{8}{10}$
$10\overline{)588}$

$571\frac{4}{8}$
$8\overline{)4572}$

$795\frac{5}{6}$
$6\overline{)4775}$

$887\frac{1}{4}$
$4\overline{)3549}$

$2409\frac{2}{3}$
$3\overline{)7229}$

Continue...

$$925 \frac{3}{7}$$
$$7 \overline{)6478}$$

$$397 \frac{7}{9}$$
$$9 \overline{)3580}$$

$$7063 \frac{2}{5}$$
$$5 \overline{)35317}$$

$$4567 \frac{8}{10}$$
$$10 \overline{)45678}$$

Shelly installs sand boxes in yards around her neighborhood. Last month, she installed 6 sand boxes. Overall, she used 94,585 pounds of sand. How many pounds of sand did she use in each sandbox?

$$15764 \frac{1}{6} \, pounds \, of \, sand$$
$$6 \overline{)94585}$$

42

LESSON 42 WORKSHEET C

1.
$$\begin{array}{r} 228 \\ 7\,\overline{)1600} \\ \underline{14} \\ 20 \\ \underline{14} \\ 60 \\ \underline{56} \\ 4 \end{array}$$

228 cases per community   **7 cases left over**

2.   10 pizzas x 8 slices = 80 slices   80 slices divided by 9 players
$$\begin{array}{r} 8 \\ 9\,\overline{)80} \\ \underline{72} \\ 8 \end{array}$$

The coach kept 8 slices for himself.

3. $100 divided by 3 kids   **$33.00 each** $\frac{1}{3}$ *dollars left over*
$$\begin{array}{r} 33 \\ 3\,\overline{)100} \\ \underline{9} \\ 10 \\ \underline{9} \\ 1 \end{array}$$

4.   155 brownies + 18 brownies = 173 brownies. Times 2 = 346 smaller brownies
346 brownies divided by 8 brownies = **43 boxes with two brownies left over**

5. $7{,}643 \div 2 = 3{,}821\frac{1}{2}$

6. $17{,}954 \div 14 = 1{,}282\frac{6}{14}$

7. $605{,}221 \div 3 = 201{,}740\frac{1}{3}$

8. $32{,}957 \div 8 = 4{,}119\frac{5}{8}$

9. $47{,}521 \div 12 = 3{,}960\frac{1}{12}$

10. $727{,}001 \div 22 = 33{,}045\frac{11}{22}$

43

```
      299.66          124.25          74.8          127.833
   3) 899.00       4) 497.00      5) 374.0       6) 767.000
      6               4              35              6
      29              09             24              16
      27              8              20              12
      29              17             40              47
      27              16             40              42
      20              10             0               50
      18              8                              48
      20              20                             20
      18              20                             18
      2               0                              20
```

```
      122.142857          92.125          43.22          361.5
   7) 855.0000000      8) 737.000      9) 389.00      2) 723.0
      7                   72              36              6
      15                  17              29              12
      14                  16              27              12
      15                  10              20              03
      14                  8               18              2
      10                  20              20              10
      7                   16              18              10
      30                  40              2               0
      28                  40
      20                  0
      14
      60
      56
      40
      35
      50
      49
      10
      7
```

```
      1391.2              555.5              2856.66            2990.5
  5) 6956.0          4) 2222.0          3) 8570.00         2) 5981.0
     5                  20                  6                  4
     19                 22                  25                 19
     15                 20                  24                 18
     45                 22                  17                 18
     45                 20                  15                 18
     06                 20                  20                 01
      5                 20                  18                  0
     10                  0                  20                 10
     10                                     18                 10
      0                                     20                  0
                                            18
                                            20
```

```
      813.81             412.0833           583.375            931.22
 11)8952.000         12)4945.0000        8) 4667.000        9) 8381.00
    88                  48                  40                 81
    15                  14                  66                 28
    11                  12                  64                 27
    42                  25                  27                 11
    33                  24                  24                  9
    90                  10                  30                 20
    88                   0                  24                 18
    20                 100                  60                 20
    11                  96                  56                 18
    90                  40                  40                  2
    88                  36                  40
     2                  40                   0
```

Since $9,570 ends in a zero, I know that 10 will go into 9,570 evenly. So now I know that something times 10 will equal 9,570. I also know that any number times 10 will be that number with a zero at the end, so it must be 957 x 10. Maggie's payments need to be $957 each to have it paid off in 10 equal payments.

```
      55.5              68.66             135.66            91.75
2 ) 111.0         3 ) 206.00        6 ) 814.00        4 ) 367.00
    10                18                6                 36
    11                26                21                07
    10                24                18                4
    10                20                34                30
     0                18                30                28
                      20                40                20
                      18                36                20
                       2                40                 0
                                        36
                                         4


    43.875            136.8             85.44            97.714285
8 ) 351.00        5 ) 684.0         9 ) 769.00        7 ) 684.000000
    32                5                 72                63
    31                18                49                54
    24                15                45                49
    70                34                40                50
    64                30                36                49
    60                40                40                10
    56                40                36                 7
    40                                  40                30
    40                                                    28
                                                          20
                                                          14
                                                          60
                                                          56
                                                          40
                                                          35
                                                          50
```

Continue...

```
       273.25              419.833            584.428571            2345.375
    4 ) 1093.00         6 ) 2519.000       7 ) 4091.000000      8 ) 18763.000
       8                   24                 35                   16
       29                  11                 59                   27
       28                  6                  56                   24
        13                  59                 31                   36
        12                  54                 28                   32
         10                 50                  30                   43
          8                 48                  28                   40
          20                 20                  20                   30
          20                 18                  14                   24
                             20                 60                   60
                             18                 56                   56
                                               40                   40
                                               35                   40
                                                50
                                                49
                                                 10
                                                  7
                                                  3
```

Continue...

```
      886.22              532.45              647.6             1526.58‾33‾
  9 ) 7976.00         11 ) 5857.00        5 ) 3238.0         12 ) 8319.0000
      72                  55                  30                  12
      77                  35                  23                  63
      72                  33                  20                  60
      56                  27                  38                  31
      54                  22                  35                  24
      20                  50                  30                  79
      18                  44                  30                  72
      20                  60                   0                  70
      18                  55                                     60
       2                   5                                    100
                                                                 96
                                                                 40
                                                                 36
                                                                 40
```

Jamie, Joe, Danny, and Erin found a pot of gold worth $2,910. If they split the gold equally with each other, how much money would each of their share of gold be worth? **$727.50**

```
        727.50
  4 ) 2910.00
      28
      11
       8
      30
      28
      20
      20
```

Give two answers for each division problem. One answer should have a fractional remainder, and the other answer should be written with a decimal number. The first one is done for you.

ANSWERS

Decimal Number   Fractional Remainder

1.
$$\begin{array}{r} 637.75 \\ \hline 12)\overline{7653.00} \\ \underline{72} \\ 45 \\ \underline{36} \\ 93 \\ \underline{84} \\ 9\,0 \\ \underline{84} \\ 60 \end{array}$$

637.75 $637\dfrac{9}{12}$

2.
$$\begin{array}{r} 978.25 \\ \hline 16\,)\,\overline{15652.00} \\ \underline{144} \\ 125 \\ \underline{112} \\ 132 \\ \underline{128} \\ 40 \\ \underline{32} \\ 80 \\ \underline{80} \\ 0 \end{array}$$

978.25 $978\dfrac{4}{16}$

Continue...

ANSWERS

Decimal Number   Fractional Remainder

$$5438.5$$

3. $24\,)\,130524.0$ $5,438.50$ $5,438\,\dfrac{12}{24}$

      120

      105

       96

       92

       72

      204

      192

      120

      120

$$6301.2$$

4. $20\,)\,126024.0$ 6301.2 $6,302\,\dfrac{4}{20}$

      120

       60

       60

      024

       20

       40

       40

        0

Continue...

103

5.

$$\begin{array}{r} 9579.1 \\ \hline 10\ )\ 95791.0 \\ \underline{90} \\ 57 \\ \underline{50} \\ 79 \\ \underline{70} \\ 91 \\ \underline{90} \\ 10 \\ \underline{10} \\ 0 \end{array}$$

9,579.1

$9,579 \frac{1}{10}$

6.

$$\begin{array}{r} 47439.05 \\ \hline 40\ )\ 1897562.00 \\ \underline{160} \\ 297 \\ \underline{280} \\ 175 \\ \underline{160} \\ 156 \\ \underline{120} \\ 362 \\ \underline{360} \\ 200 \\ \underline{200} \\ 0 \end{array}$$

47,439.05

$47,439 \frac{2}{40}$

104

43a

```
        3                      103                  31.1809523              1 1.4
  311)933                724)74572          105)3274.0000000         695)7923.0
      933                    724                315                      695
        0                   2172                124                      973
                            2172                105                      695
                               0                190                     2780
                                               105                     2780
                                               850                        0
                                               840
                                              1000
                                               945
                                               550
                                               525
                                               250
                                               210
                                               400
                                               315
                                               850
```

```
         347                 282                  124                   52
     9 ─────             5 ─────            253 ─────             664 ─────
         402                 589                  193                  120

  402)3965             589)3227            193)48953            120)79732
      3618                 2945                386                  720
       347                  282               1035                  773
                                               965                  720
                                               703                  532
                                               579                  480
                                               124                   52
```

Laney saved up $12,448 for college. Each class costs $389. How many classes can Laney pay for with the money she has saved?

32 classes

```
   389)12448
       1167
        778
```

43a

```
              6.04                    13                 32.33                11.11
      125 ) 755.00           698 ) 9074         150 ) 4850.00         9 ) 100.00
            750                     698                 450                 9
            500                    2094                 350                10
            500                    2094                 300                 9
                                                        500                10
                                                        450                 9
                                                        500                10
                                                                            9
```

```
                    36                      22                     16                      61
            102 357                 819 195                76 409               1759 582
      357 ) 36450             195 ) 159727          409 ) 31100           582 ) 1023799
            357                     1560                  2863                  582
            750                      372                  2470                 4417
            714                      195                  2454                 4074
             36                     1777                    16                 3439
                                    1755                                       2910
                                      22                                       5299
                                                                               5238
                                                                                 61
```

```
             30 R 9                    316 R 58               456 R 47
      33 ) 999               410 ) 129,618          91 ) 41,543
            99                      1230                   364
            09                       661                   514
                                     410                   455
                                    2518                   593
                                    2460                   546
                                      58                    47
```

106

43a

1.
```
        93.545
   7 ) 654.815
      63
      ‾‾
      24
      21
      ‾‾
      38
      35
      ‾‾
      31
      28
      ‾‾
      35
      35
      ‾‾
```

Your Answer →

```
    93.545
  ×      7
  ‾‾‾‾‾‾‾
   654.815
```

2.
```
       207.89
  18 ) 3742.02
      36
      ‾‾
      142
      126
      ‾‾‾
      160
      144
      ‾‾‾
      162
      162
      ‾‾‾
```

Your Answer →

```
    207.89
  ×     18
  ‾‾‾‾‾‾‾
   166312
   207890
  ‾‾‾‾‾‾‾
   3742.02
```

3.
```
          8087.43
  631 ) 5103168.33
       5048
       ‾‾‾‾
       5516
       5048
       ‾‾‾‾
       4688
       4417
       ‾‾‾‾
       2713
       2524
       ‾‾‾‾
       1893
```

```
      8087.43
    ×     631
  ‾‾‾‾‾‾‾‾‾
    808743
   24262290
  485245800
  ‾‾‾‾‾‾‾‾‾
  5,103,168.33
```

1.
```
              501.11
      36.)18040.00
          180
          040
           36
           40
           36
           40
```

2.
```
             200.
     607)121400.
         1214
           00
```

3.
```
          10205.55
      9)91850.
        9
        01
         0
        18
        18
        0050
          45
          50
```

4.
```
           1243.33
     75)93250.00
        75
        182
        150
        325
        300
        250
        225
        250
        225
        250
```

5.
```
          9425.
     8)75400.
       72
       34
       32
       20
       16
       40
```

6.
```
          4.54
     12)54.48
        48
        64
        60
        48
```

Will and Jamie have been saving quarters for a year. They now have $26.50 worth of quarters saved up. How many quarters do they have? If they split up the quarters evenly, how many will each person get?

106. Total quarters.
```
25)2650.
   25
   150
```

```
     53
  2)106
```

53 quarters for Jamie

53 quarters for Will

LESSON 44 WORKSHEET B

```
        2.                    1.7                  1400.                  25.
39 ) 78.            152 ) 258.4          703 ) 984200.        1061 ) 26525.
     78                    152                  703                  2122
      0                   1064                 2812                 5305
                          1064                 2812                 5305
                             0                    0                    0
```

```
     24190.                  20.                  210.                 839.
03 ) 72570.         981 ) 19620.          36 ) 7560.          812 ) 681268.
     6                    1962                  72                  6496
    12                      00                  36                  3166
    12                                          36                  2436
     05                                          0                  7308
      3                                                             7308
     27                                                                0
     27
     00
```

```
   1448.0
2 ) 2896.0
```

1,448 text messages

44

1.   24 Cans of sauce

2.   330 boards

3.   5 truckloads of dirt

4.   30 books

5.   26 bolts

6.   12 toys

7. $274.35 per day

8.   800 balloons

Round each number to the nearest whole dollar.

1.	$55.67 = **$56**	6.	$411.05 = **$411**
2.	$92.54 = **$93**	7.	$0.55 = **$1**
3.	$102.02 = **$102**	8.	$23.75 = **$24**
4.	$33.99 = **$34**	9.	$7.29 = **$7**
5.	$112.51 = **$113**	10.	$3.50 = **$4**

Round each number to the nearest hundredth.

11.	.3045 = **.30**	16.	5790.6421269 = **5790.64**
12.	5.067 = **5.07**	17	.999 = **1.00**
13.	42.002 = **42.00**	18.	.0005 = **.00**
14.	.9925 = **.99**	19.	.1099 = **.11**
15.	.0321 = **.03**	20	76.990 = **76.99**

Round each number to the nearest tenth.

21.	.677 = **.7**	26.	.85 = **.9**
22.	1.12 = **1.1**	27.	.102 = **.1**
23.	14.556 = **14.6**	28.	9.73 = **9.7**
24.	72.007 = **72.0**	29.	.71 = **.7**
25.	99.99 = **100.0**	30.	.09742 = **.1**

It cost approximately $14 per person

Round each number to the nearest whole number, tenth, and hundredth. The first one is done for you.

NUMBER	WHOLE NUMBER	TENTH	HUNDREDTH
0.839	1	0.8	0.84
2.053	2	2.1	2.05
60.618	61	60.6	60.62
5.044	5	5.0	5.04
0.999	1	1.0	1.00
1.705	2	1.7	1.71
41.773	42	41.8	41.77
6.952	7	7.0	6.95
0.276	0	.3	.28
3.516	4	3.5	3.52
8.009	8	8.0	8.01
7.237	7	7.2	7.24
1.345	1	1.3	1.35
9482.5217	9483	9482.5	9482.52

$$\begin{array}{r} 3.75 \\ 8\overline{)30.0} \\ \underline{24} \\ 60 \\ \underline{56} \\ 40 \\ \underline{40} \end{array}$$ She will need 4 balls of yarn.

45

1. 8.03 7.57
    <u> 8 </u> = <u> 8 </u>

2. 5.09 4.43
    <u> 5 </u> > <u> 4 </u>

3. 6.97 7.60
    <u> 7 </u> < <u> 8 </u>

4. 12.4 13.04
    <u> 12 </u> < <u> 13 </u>
112

5. 0.8 0.49
    <u> 1 </u> > <u> 0 </u>

6. 111.1 112.01
    <u>   </u> **111** <
    112

7. 0.967 0.982
    <u> 1.0 </u> = <u> 1.0 </u>

8. 1.654 1.641
    <u> 1.7 </u> > <u> 1.6 </u>

9. 44.067 43.089
    <u> **44.1** </u> > <u> **43.1** </u>

10. 18.053 18.049
     <u> **18.1** </u> > <u> **18.0** </u>

11. 297.857 287.81
     <u> **297.9** </u> > <u> **287.8** </u>

12. 3.111 3.119
     <u> **3.1** </u> = <u> **3.1** </u>

13. 1,447.92

14. 283.47

15. 14,473.68

13.
```
        1447.924
  53 ) 76740.000
       53
       237
       212
        254
        212
         420
         371
         490
         477
          130
          106
          240
```

14.
```
       283.473
  19 ) 5386.000
       38
       158
       152
        66
        57
        90
        76
       140
       133
        70
        57
        13
```

15.
```
        14473.683
  38) 550000.000
      38
      170
      152
       180
       152
        280
        266
        140
        114
         260
         228
         320
         304
         160
```

Above Average Dice Game

RULES:
1.   The first player rolls two dice. Multiply those two numbers together. That is your score for the round.
2.   Players take turns rolling the dice until each player has three scores.
3.   Each player adds their scores together and divides by three to get their average score for that round.
4.   Play three rounds and then get your average score from those scores. The LOWEST score wins. There is a scorecard for Player 2 on the next page.

PLAYER 1		SCORE
Round 1 1st Roll Score		
2nd Roll Score		
3rd Roll Score		
Add three scores		
Divide by 3		
AVERAGE SCORE Round 1	⟶	
Round 2 1st Roll Score		
2nd Roll Score		
3rd Roll Score		
Add three scores		
Divide by 3		
AVERAGE SCORE Round 2	⟶	
Round 3 1st Roll Score		
2nd Roll Score		
3rd Roll Score		
Add three scores		
Divide by 3		
AVERAGE SCORE Round 3	⟶	
Add all three rounds	⟶	
Divide by 3		
FINAL SCORE		

PLAYER 2		SCORE
Round 1 1st Roll Score		
2nd Roll Score		
3rd Roll Score		
Add three scores		
Divide by 3		
AVERAGE SCORE Round 1	⟶	
Round 2 1st Roll Score		
2nd Roll Score		
3rd Roll Score		
Add three scores		
Divide by 3		
AVERAGE SCORE Round 2	⟶	
Round 3 1st Roll Score		
2nd Roll Score		
3rd Roll Score		
Add three scores		
Divide by 3		
AVERAGE SCORE Round 3	⟶	
Add all three rounds	⟶	
Divide by 3		
FINAL SCORE		

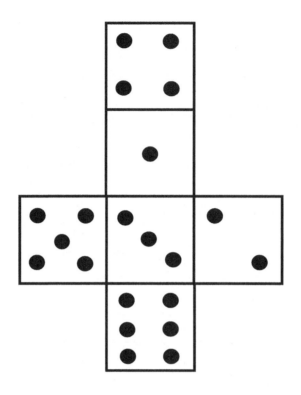

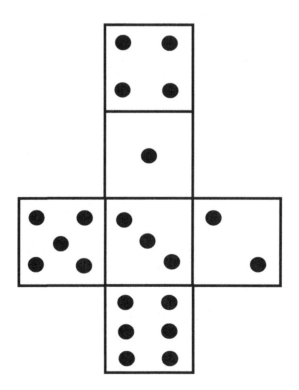

45a

1. $54 + 38 + 62 = 154 \qquad 154 \div 3 = 51.33$ *or* 51 *marbles*
2. **68.5 pounds** $\div 7 = 9.78$ **pounds**
3. What is the rare plant's average rate of growth? **7.25 feet per week**
   How much did the plant grow after one month? **29 feet**

LESSON 45A WORKSHEET C

1. $201,010
   $180,000
   $ 74,950
   $455,960 $\qquad$ $455,960 \div 5 = \$91,192$ *per day*

2. $2063.50 \div 4 = 515.875$ *miles driven per day*

3. $17.25 + 15.6 + 14.2 = 47.05 \qquad 47.05 \div 3 = 15.68\overline{33}$ *minutes*

4. $25 \times 28 = 700$
   $22 \times 27 = 594$
   $8 \times 30 = 240$
   $1 \times 51 = 51$
   $1 \times 54 = \underline{54}$
   TOTAL: $1639 \div 57$ *people* $= 28.75$ *years old*

5. $42 + 38 + 54 + 46 = 180 \qquad 180$ *points* $\div 4$ *games* $= 45$ *points per game*

6.
Monday	$1,278.45
Tuesday	$1,459.44
Wednesday	$2,007.64
Thursday	$3,590.21
Friday	$5,578.91
TOTAL	$13,914.65

   $13,914.65 \div 5 = \$2,782.93$ *average per day*

Review

1. 11 x 17 = **187** 2. 12 x 8 = **96** 3. 14 x 9.5 = **133** 4. 1725 x 10 = **17,250**
5. **2,058** 6. 35.206 7. 3,693.64 8. 339.07
9. 48 ÷ 8 = **6** 10. 81 ÷ 9 = **9** 11. 90 ÷ 18 = **5** 12. 5000 ÷ 100 = **50**

13.
$$501\tfrac{2}{8}$$
$$8\overline{)4010}$$
$$\underline{40}$$
$$010$$
$$\underline{8}$$
$$2$$

14.
$$409\tfrac{2}{5}$$
$$5\overline{)2047}$$
$$\underline{20}$$
$$047$$
$$\underline{45}$$
$$2$$

15.
$$85\tfrac{5}{7}$$
$$7\overline{)600}$$
$$\underline{56}$$
$$40$$
$$\underline{35}$$
$$5$$

16.
$$702\tfrac{4}{12}$$
$$12\overline{)8428}$$
$$\underline{84}$$
$$028$$
$$\underline{24}$$
$$4$$

17.
$$75.125$$
$$8\overline{)601.00}$$
$$\underline{56}$$
$$41$$
$$\underline{40}$$
$$10$$
$$\underline{8}$$
$$20$$
$$\underline{16}$$
$$40$$

18.
$$3.\overline{03}$$
$$99\overline{)300.00}$$
$$\underline{297}$$
$$300$$

19.
$$507.2$$
$$5\overline{)2536.0}$$
$$\underline{25}$$
$$036$$
$$\underline{35}$$
$$10$$

20.
$$1.\overline{33}$$
$$6\overline{)8.00}$$
$$\underline{6}$$
$$20$$
$$\underline{18}$$
$$20$$

21.   12 = 2, 3, 4, 6   18 = 2, 3, 6, 9   20 = 2, 4, 5, 10

22. 40,559   Thousands
23. 10   Ones
24. 88,039,544   Hundred thousands
25. 108,365,291   Ten millions
26. 70,335,157,482   Billions   Continue...

118

Review

27.
$$\begin{array}{r} 13 \text{ R } 70 \\ 110 \overline{)\ 1500} \\ \underline{110} \\ 400 \\ \underline{330} \\ 70 \end{array}$$

$$\begin{array}{r} 9 \text{ R } 60 \\ 160 \overline{)\ 1500} \\ \underline{1440} \\ 60 \end{array}$$

$$\begin{array}{r} 6 \\ 250 \overline{)\ 1500} \\ \underline{1500} \\ 0 \end{array}$$

Frank should buy 6 packs of 250 balls.

28.
$$\begin{array}{r} 1.55 \\ 24 \overline{)\ 37.20} \\ \underline{24} \\ 132 \\ \underline{120} \\ 120 \\ \underline{120} \end{array}$$

$$\begin{array}{r} 1.52 \\ 26 \overline{)\ 39.52} \\ \underline{26} \\ 135 \\ \underline{130} \\ 52 \\ \underline{52} \end{array}$$

The cupcakes at Margie's Cupcakes are cheapest at $1.52 each.

29. $115 + 96 + 174 + 138 = 523$ $523 \div 4 = 130 \, R3$

Jamie wrote an average of 130 words per week.

30. $3 + 1 + 0 + 2 + 5 + 3 + 1 = 15 \, shooting \, stars$

$15 \, stars \div 7 \, days = an \, average \, of \, 2 \, shooting \, stars \, per \, day.$

TEST

1. 6 x 4 = **24**   2. 9 x 80 = **720**   3. 200 x 8 = **1,600**

4. 8,342   5. 7,009   6. 84.327
    x 546   x 769   x .0547
    50,052   63,081   590,289
    333,680   420,540   3,373,080
    4,171,000   4,906,300   42,163,500
    4,554,732   **5,389,921**   **4.6126869**

Use < and > signs to show which number is bigger.

7. 7.123 < 7.231   8. .045 < .054   9. .1 > .01

                    9   **90**   **931**
10. 5) 45   11. 8) 720   12. 6) 5586

Divide the following. Turn any remainders into a fraction.

        48 1/7   **943 5/9**   **1253 2/5**
13. 7) 337   14. 9) 8492   15. 5) 6267
     28   81   5
     57   39   12
     56   36   10
      1   32   26
                         27   25
                          5   17
                                             15

120

```
              2441.5                    115.9090
16.    12 ) 29298.0       17.     11 ) 1275.0000
          24                            11
          52                            17
          48                            11
          49                            65
          48                            55
          18                           100
          12                            99
          60                           100
          60                            99
```

```
              206.092307692
18.    13 ) 2690.00000
          26
          090
           78
          120
          117
           30
           26
           40
           39
          100
           91
           90
           78
          120
          117
           30
```

121

TEST

19. $1,162,310

$$\begin{array}{r} 1162310 \\ 3\overline{)3486930} \end{array}$$

20.

$$78 - 10 = 68 \qquad 17\overline{)68}^{\,4} \qquad \text{Each student got 4 pieces of candy.}$$

21. 3 aunts x $10 = $30
    2 grandmas x $250 = $500
    1 set of parents x $500 = $500
    5 cousins x $12 = $60

    $30 + $500 + $500 +$60 = $1,090

22. 2 movie tickets x $13.00 = $26.00
    2 large popcorns x $1.75 = $ 3.50
    2 large drinks x $2.55 = $ 5.10
    4 boxes of candy x $1.25 = $ 5.00
    6 cinnamon sticks x $0.75 = $ 4.50
                                      $44.10

    $50.00 - $44.10 = $5.90   Mick has **$5.90** left over.

23. **Her mean score is 9.6**

    9.5
    9.4
    9.8
    9.9
    9.4
    9.6
    57.6

$$6\overline{)57.6}^{\,9.6}$$
$$\underline{54}$$
$$36$$

122

CHAPTER 4

WORKSHEET ANSWERS

LearnMathFastBooks.com

LESSON 46 WORKSHEET

1. 1 **inch**
2. 2 **feet**
3. 50 **yards**
4. 5 **feet**
5. 8 **inches**
6. 6 **feet** tall and 20 **yards** long
7. 12 inches = 1 **foot**
8. 3 feet = 1 **yard**
9. 1 yard - 2 feet = 1 **foot**
10. 3 **inches**
11. 65 **yards**
12. 40 **yards**
13. 50 **yard**
14. 12 feet
15. 2 **feet**
16. 3 **inches**

LESSON 46 WORKSHEET B

1. inches
2. mile
3. inches
4. 12
5. feet
6. 15 feet or 180 inches
7. feet
8. Miles
9. inches
10. Feet
11. miles
12. yard

Circle the correct answer.

 (feet)   inches

(miles)   yards

124

1.   4 feet and 6 inches

2.   4 feet and 6 inches

3.   80 inches

4.   13 x 12 inches = 156 inches   156 inches + 6 inches = 162 inches
      Yes the truck will fit in the tunnel.

5.   10 feet

6.   1,760   1760 yards
      3) 5,280

7.   34 x 12 inches = 408 inches   408 inches + 7 inches = 415 inches
      No, the boat will not fit in the driveway.

8.   2 feet 4 inches

9.   ten rows of firewood

10.   20 feet = 240 inches   90 inches + 90 inches = 180 inches.
      Yes, there will be enough room.

11.   1 mile = 5,280 feet   5 miles = 26,400 feet   5 miles = 316,800 inches

12.   7 feet and 4 inches = 88 inches   88 inches – 36 inches = 52 inches

1.   tablespoon
2.   teaspoons
3.   cup
4.   tablespoons
5.   teaspoon
6.   2 cups = 16 ounces
7.   Fluid ounce
8.   tablespoons
9.   ounces
10. ounces
11. ounces
12. 3 Tablespoons
13. Which is bigger? (7 t) or   7 T
14. ounce

LESSON 47 WORKSHEET B

1.   Tablespoons
2.   8 ounces
3.   Candace added 12 teaspoons, which is more than Phoebe added.
4.   Tablespoon
5.   teaspoon
6.   3 T = 9 teaspoons
7.   30 t = 5 fl.oz.
8.   48 ounces of flour
9.   4 ounces
10. 12 tsp. + 3 Tbls. = 7 Tbls.
11. 12 tsp. + 3 Tbls. = 3.5 fl.oz.
12. 300 fl oz – 21 fl oz = 279 fl oz.   279 fl ounces x 2 = 558 Tablespoons

1. 1 cup = 8 fl. oz. 4 cups = 32 fl. oz. There is more milk in the glass pitcher.
2. 1 cup = 8 ounces. 1 ounce = 2 tablespoons. 1 cup = 16 tablespoons.
3. 1 bottle = 2 cups. Doctors recommend drinking 4 bottles of water each day.
4. 1 tablespoon = 3 teaspoons. You should use 6 teaspoons of oil.
5. 2 fluid ounces of butter.
6. 1 cup = 8 ounces. 1 ounce = 2 tablespoons. 2 cups = 32 tablespoons of milk.
7. 1 cup of water is less than of 10 fluid ounces.
8. 9 teaspoons of vinegar are more than 1 fluid ounce of vinegar.

　　　　　6　　　+　1　　　　+ 2　　　　　　　　8 - 1

9. Six fluid ounces + 2 tablespoon + 12 teaspoons　　>　1 cup – 1 fl. oz.

　　　　　　48　　　　　　　40　　+　6

10. 48 ounces of pop　　>　　5 cups and 6 ounces of pop

（2 ounces + 5 t.) + 8　　　48　　-　36

11. 17 teaspoons + 1 cup　　<　6 cups – 36 fluid ounces

　　　　　11　　　　　8　　+　2

12. 11 ounces of gas　　>　　1 cup of gas + 12 teaspoons of gas

1. 1 gallon of milk = 4 **quarts** of milk.
2. 4 cups of water = 1 **quart** of water.
3. 2 cups of broth = 1 **pint** of broth.
4. **3 quarts**
5. 1 cup of water – 2 tablespoons = **7 fluid ounces**.
6. **8 glasses**
7. How many cups are in 1 gallon? **16 cups**
8. How many ounces are in 1 gallon? **128 ounces**
9. How many tablespoons are in 1 gallon? **256 tablespoons**
10. **9 ounces**
11. **8 times**
12. How many teaspoons are in a gallon? **768 teaspoons**

LESSON 48 WORKSHEET B

1. 16 fluid ounces
2. 2 cups
3. 43,200 quarts.
4. 1 gallon = 16 cups.
5. 2 cups = 16 fluid ounces.
6. 1 pint - 6 tablespoons = 13 fl. oz.
7. 27 cookies
8. 7 quarts
9. 5 gallons = 640 fl. oz.
10. Half a gallon is 2 quarts, 4 pints, or 8 cups.
11. 256 Tablespoons
12. 3,800 gallons – 3,350 gallons = 450 gallons   1 gallon = 4 quarts
    450 gallons x 4 = 1800 quarts

1. $3.28 \div 4 = .82$ $0.82 per quart

2. $2.88 \div 4 = .72$ $0.72 per cup

3. $.83 \times 2 = 1.66$ $1.66 per quart

4. 8 ounces

5. 1 quart = 32 ounces   It will take seven more hours to fill the container.

6. There are four cups of paint left in the can.
   That is equal to 2 pints or 1 quart.

7. 2 cups of water, 4 cups of flour and 12 cups of milk.

49

1. Angel's new baby weighed 7 **pounds** and 6 **ounces** when he was born.
2. The big truck weighed over 2 **tons**.
3. Pat bought 3 **pounds** of bananas at the store.
4. The cell phone is nice and lightweight. It only weighs 7 **ounces**.
5. Sherry went on a diet and lost 10 **pounds**.
6. Lynda shoveled over 200 **pounds** of dirt into the garden.
7. What is the difference between an ounce and a fluid ounce?
    A fluid ounces measures liquid.   An ounce measures weight.
8. How many ounces are in a half pound? **8 ounces**
9. An apple weighs 18 ounces. Is it more or less than a pound?
    More than a pound, it is 1 pound 2 ounces.
10. 1 pound – 12 ounces = **4 ounces.**
11. 1 ton – 1999 pounds and 2 ounces = **14 ounces.**
12. **30 pounds and 2 ounces.**
13. **800 pounds.**
14. **Josh's computer weighs 208 ounces, his weighs more.**

LESSON 49 WORKSHEET B

1. 14,000 pounds

2. $$\begin{array}{r} 3 \\ 225 \overline{)\,675} \\ \underline{675} \\ 0 \end{array}$$ 3 pounds of lemons

3. 165 tons
4. They weigh the same.
5   1 pound = 16 ounces
6. pounds
7. 9,898 pounds   Continue...

130

LESSON 49 WORKSHEET B CONTINUED

8. Ounces
9. Pounds
10. George's piggy bank weighs more.
11. 320 ounces
12. 1 ton = 2000 pounds = 32,000 ounces
13. 465,002,500 pounds

LESSON 49 WORKSHEET C

1. 1600 pounds
2. 9 ounces
3. 12 ounces
4. 2,800 pounds
5. 2 pounds
6. 130 pounds and 9 ounces
7. $11
8. 4 truckloads
9. 8 fluid ounces/16 ounces
10. $0.75 per ounce

Review

1. My dog is 24 inches tall. That's **two** feet. He weighs 75 **pounds** and 6 **ounces**.
2. My snake is 2 yards long. That's **six** feet.
3. A mile is 5280 feet long. How many yards is that? **1760 yards**
4. 4 cups = **two** pints = 1 **quart**.
5. 2 cups = **16** fluid ounces.
6. An elephant weighs about 4 tons. That's **8,000** pounds.
7. Isaac's bike is 3 **feet** tall. He rode his bike 2 **miles** to his favorite pizzeria. He bought a 16 **inch** wide pizza and bought a 12 **fluid ounce** can of soda.
8. 3 **teaspoons** = 1 tablespoon.
9. 2 **tablespoons** = 1 fluid ounce.
10. The distance from Chicago to New York city is 789 **miles**.
11. 16 ounces x 7 = 112 ounces, so **Kim weighed more**.
12. 4 **cups** = 1 quart
13. 4 quarts = 1 **gallon**
14. 5 tablespoons - 9 teaspoons = **2** tablespoons
15. 1 gallon - 2 quarts - 1 pint = **six** cups.
16. 1 ton - 316 pounds + 64 ounces = **1,688** pounds.
17. 5,207 pounds = 83,312 ounces
18. 20,000 quarts of milk and about 7 tons of cereal.
19. 3 quarts or 12 cups
20. 8 miles or 14,080 yards

TEST

1. 1 cup = **8** fluid ounces.

2. 1 yard = **3** feet.

3. 1 pound = **16** ounces.

4. Make this a true statement: **4** cups = **32** ounces = 2 pints.

5. I stepped on the scale and found out I gained 7 **pounds**, so I drank 2 **pints (or cups, or quarts)** of water and ran 2 **miles**.

6. I took an ice cube out of my drink. It measured 1 **inch** tall and 1 **inch** wide.
   I put it on a scale and it weighed 6 **ounces**. Once the ice cube melted, I measured the water. It measured 1 **fluid ounce**.

7. **A mile**

8. **An inch**

9. **A ton**

10. **A gallon**

11. **Pounds**

12. It was about 12 **inches** long. Next to it was a 12 **ounce** can of pop.
    The ice sculpture looked like it must have weighed over 50 **pounds**.

13. 12 inches = 1 **foot**.

14. 5280 feet = 1 **mile**.

15. 8 fluid ounces = 1 **cup**.

16. **The directions say to use 1 tsp per cup. Virginia needs to make 3 quarts, which is the same as 12 cups. To make 12 cups of coffee we need 12 teaspoons. 1 tablespoon equals 3 teaspoons, so we need 4 tablespoons of coffee. There are 8 ounces/cup so she will need 96 ounces of water.**

17. **1 mile equals 5280 feet. The taxi drove 2 miles. $3.23 x 2 = $6.46 The taxi ride cost $6.46.**

18. 2 yards equals 6 feet. He walked 6 feet away from the door. The butterfly made him go back 4 feet, so now he is 2 feet from   the door. The dog made him go 18" or 1 $\frac{1}{2}$ feet away from the door. **He is now 3 $\frac{1}{2}$ feet from the door.**

19. 2 quarts is half a gallon, so we need to use half the fruit punch mix, which is a half cup or **4 ounces**.

TEST

20. When Keegan was a puppy she weighed 23 ounces. Now she weighs 18 pounds and 4 ounces. How much weight has Keegan gained?

    18 pounds = 288 ounces   288 ounces + 4 ounces = 292 ounces
    292 ounces - 23 ounces = 269 ounces = 16 pounds and 13 ounces

21. The doorway opening is 32 inches. How many feet and inches is that?

    $32 \div 12 = 2\,R\,8$ **2 feet and 8 inches**

22. Patty made a fruit salad. She added 9 ounces of blueberries, 1 pound of cantaloupe, 10 ounces of raspberries, 14 ounces of strawberries, and 1 pound of grapes. How much does the fruit salad weigh?

Blueberries:	**9 ounces**
Cantaloupe:	**16 ounces**
Raspberries:	**10 ounces**
Strawberries:	**14 ounces**
Grapes:	**16 ounces**
TOTAL:	**65 ounces or 4 pounds and 1 ounce**

23. How many yards are in a mile?

    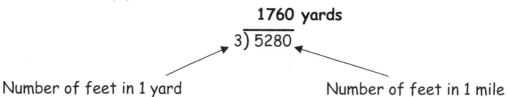

    Number of feet in 1 yard   Number of feet in 1 mile

FINAL TEST

1.   9 + 8 = **17**   2.   14 + 7 = **21**   3. 28 + 6 = **34**   4. 117 + 5 = **122**

5.   33.67   6.   41.07   7.   30.0   8.   99
    + 22.70   + 21.90   + 27.5   52
    56.37   **62.97**   **57.5**   244
                                               + 81
                                             476

9.   15 - 8 = **7**   10. 24 - 6 = **18**   11. 40 - 7 = **33**   12.   12 - 9 = **3**

13.   1000   14.   924   15.   25.12   16.   13.953
    -874   - 88   - 7.13   - 2.1
    126   **836**   **17.99**   **11.853**

17.   8 x 4 = **32**   18.   7 x 6 = **42**   19.   3 x 7 = **21**   20.   9 x 7 = **63**

21.   23 x 11 = **253**   22. 12 x 4 = **48**   23. 13 x 3 = **39** 24.16 x 5 = **80**

25.   27.8   26.   765.2   27.   15706.1   28.   9876
    x .21   x 4.5   x 358.7   x 378
    278   38260   1099427   79008
    5560   306080   12564880   691320
    5.838   3,443.40   78530500   2962800
                          471183000   3,733,128
                          5,633,778.07

29.   54 ÷ 9 = **6**   30.   64 ÷ 8 = **8**   31.   48 ÷ 6 = **8**   32.   32 ÷ 8 = **4**

TEST

```
         816                189                32.15              71.72
33.  4)3264       34.  3)567      35.  8)257.20      36.  9)645.48
         32                 3                24                 63
         06                26                17                 15
          4                24                16                  9
         24                27                12                 64
                                              8                 63
                                             40                 18
```

```
            1                 2                 4                 1
        908 7            157 5            299 9            864 2
37.  7)6357       38.  5)787      39.  9)2695       40.  2)1729
        63                 5                18                 16
        05                28                89                 12
         0                25                81                 12
        57                37                85                 09
        56                35                81                  8
         1                 2                 4                  1
```

```
        33.66             52.66              20              2.857142
41.  3)101.00     42.  9)474.00    43.  16)320      44.  7)20.000000
         9                45                                 14
        11                24                                 60
         9                18                                 56
        20                60                                 40
        18                54                                 35
        20                60                                 50
                                                             49
                                                             10
                                                              7
                                                             30
                                                             28
                                                             20
```

136

Round the following numbers to the nearest hundredth:

45. 45.981 = **45.98**   46. 53.4873 = **53.49**   47. 76.1687 = **76.17**

Round the following numbers to the nearest whole number:

48. 65.4767 = **65**   49. 942.15852 = **942**   50. 76.05 = **76**

Which column is the 5 in?

51.	954	Tens
52.	576	Hundreds
53.	5,218	Thousands
54.	50,236	Ten thousands
55.	15	Ones
56.	539,789,668	Hundred Millions
57.	25,000,000	Millions
58.	58,963,880	Ten millions
59.	89.05	Hundredths
60.	978.005	Thousandths
61.	16.50	Tenths

Made in the USA
Coppell, TX
06 July 2025

51516515R00077